BUSINESS
WOULD BE EASY
IF IT WASN'T FOR PEOPLE

Business Would Be Easy... If It Wasn't For People

By Ruben Buell

First Edition

Cover design by Ruben Buell

This is a work of nonfiction. The stories and reflections are based on real experiences, but identifying details may have been changed to protect privacy.

To Jennifer, who keeps me grounded, sharp, and (mostly) humble.

To my kids, the reason I care about the future of work and the people in it.

To the colleagues who challenged me, the mentors who guided me, and the wild personalities who gave me endless stories, you helped write this more than you know.

To Uncle Mel, without your guidance there would be no book.

And to my mom, who taught me everything about love, resilience, and the art of the side-eye.

INTRODUCTION

Let's just call it what it is. People are the hardest part of business. Not marketing. Not strategy. Not the tech stack or the budget. It's the people. The ones you manage, the ones you work for, the ones who derail meetings, miss deadlines, or send you 47 messages before noon. And sometimes, the hardest person to manage… is you. Especially if you don't think you're part of the problem.

This book isn't about blaming others. It's about recognizing that most of the pain in the workplace, like confusion, drama, burnout, missed deadlines, and toxic culture, doesn't come from some external boogeyman. It comes from us. From our egos, fears, and inability to communicate like adults when we're stressed, tired, or just really annoyed that the new hire microwaved fish again.

AI is Coming for Your Job

If you're a brilliant coder but a nightmare to work with, AI's going to eat your lunch. If you're a hyper-efficient operator but no one trusts you, you'll be automated out faster than you can say "ChatGPT."

The future doesn't belong to the smartest or the most technical. It belongs to the people who can *lead*, *connect*, and *collaborate*.

That's why this book matters. It's not about fixing others. It's about seeing your role clearly, and doing the work to lead better, grow faster, and suck less.

The First Time I Realized I Was the Problem

I've been managing people in one form or another since 1991, though I didn't know it at the time. That summer, I put together my first band. I was 17, wrote all the songs and led the band. We practiced every Sunday. One weekend, I had my first real experience with beer, a six-pack of Miller Genuine Draft. The next morning I was hugging the toilet and calling the band to cancel practice.

That was it, one hung-over teenager, one missed rehearsal, and I knew I had let the dream down.

That moment stuck with me. Even then, I understood: *If you say that something matters to you, you don't get to disappear when it's inconvenient.* Leadership starts with showing up. You don't inspire a team by barking orders. You do it by owning the dream harder than anyone else, and pushing through the days you'd rather be horizontal. That morning was my first taste of failure as a leader, and the beginning of an over three-decade stretch of intense personal accountability.

Sometimes, people are the problem. Sometimes, that target is squarely on you.

Business Would Be Easy If It Wasn't for People is part wake-up call, part survival guide. It's built from decades of experience leading companies big and small, building technology from scratch, scaling teams, navigating toxic cultures, and figuring out what actually works when it comes to managing people. I've been the CTO, the CEO, the guy pulling all-nighters to keep the servers running. I've worked with geniuses, narcissists, ghosters, gaslighters, and a few truly incredible people who make all the madness worth it.

This book is for you if:

- You've ever wanted to strangle your coworker over a passive-aggressive email.

- You manage people and feel like no leadership book has prepared you for this much chaos.

- You're looking to lead or move into management and have *no idea what the fuck that actually means.*

- You're already managing a big team and want to understand how to *wield the chaos* just a little better, maybe even (God forbid) remove some of it.

- You *are* the chaos (and you're finally ready to suck less).

- You believe in growth, even if it means calling yourself out first.

It's divided into three parts:

1. People Suck

This section holds up the mirror, not to everyone else, but to *you.* We start by owning the fact that we all contribute to dysfunction. It's about ego, fear, empathy, and the uncomfortable truth that personal growth starts with personal responsibility. If you want to lead people, you need to understand what makes them (and you) tick, and what makes us spiral.

2. Navigating the Work Environment

Now that you've accepted that people (including you) suck, we'll talk about how to survive, and thrive, in the wild terrain of the workplace. This is where we get into emotional intelligence, communication, accountability, collaboration, and boundaries. Basically, how to not implode... or make everyone else want to quit.

3. Bring It All Together

This is where the transformation happens. We connect the dots, build on the insights, and turn "not sucking" into a way of life. You'll learn how to lead, support, and grow into someone people actually *want* to work with, even when shit hits the fan. It's about structure, intention, and understanding how your behavior shapes your team's results.

So here's the deal:

By the time you finish this book, you'll walk away with something most people never bother to earn, *self-awareness*, *clarity*, and a *real strategy* for working with people, (including yourself). You'll learn how to lead without micromanaging, collaborate without losing your mind, and build a team that actually *functions*.

Not perfectly. Not without hard days. But better, consistently, intentionally, and with a hell of a lot less drama.

This is your invitation to level up, not just as a leader, but as a person who *gets it*.

Let's get to work.

CHAPTER 1: PEOPLE SUCK

Let's start with the truth: **people suck**.

And I don't mean "other people." I mean all of us. You. Me. That guy in IT. Your boss. Your client. Your intern. Everyone.

Not always, not completely. But often enough, especially at work, that they become the biggest reason why businesses stall, teams break down, and promising leaders burn out.

Projects don't fail because of bad ideas. They fail because people can't communicate, won't take responsibility, or are too busy protecting their egos to focus on the actual goal. The most complicated part of business isn't product or profit. It's people.

You Know This Already

You've seen examples of this play out a hundred times:

- The teammate who can't take feedback without spiraling.

- The manager who won't make a decision because someone *might* get upset.

- The employee who shows up every day but left mentally six months ago.

- The CEO with the ego of a god and the emotional intelligence of a doorknob.

And if we're being honest, you've probably been one of those people too. I know I have.

The Time I Got Told to Fuck Off (and Deserved It)

Early in my career, I co-founded a company called Rose Software. I was 19 at the time, running a team of developers, most of them friends from high school. I had a vision, I had energy, and I had a problem: I couldn't let go.

One day, my partner Dave was on the phone with a client, walking them through an issue. I was listening to the call from across the room. Being the "helpful" micromanager I was back then, I kept whispering things to him:

"Tell them this."
"No, say it this way."
"Wait, ask them about this too."

I thought I was being useful. What I was actually doing was undermining him and driving him insane. After a few minutes, he snapped. He put his hand over the receiver, turned and said, "Would you fuck off?"

It stunned me. I needed it. He was right.

That moment taught me one of the most important lessons in leadership:
Let people do the job you hired them to do.

Even if they don't do it exactly the way *you* would. Even if you think you could do it better or faster. Your job isn't to puppet them; it's to build a system that works without your constant interference.

And if you don't trust the person to handle it? That's a hiring problem, not a coaching opportunity.

We're Wired for Dysfunction

Here's the uncomfortable truth: we're not naturally wired for harmony. We're wired to protect ourselves, seek validation, avoid pain, and survive whatever social hierarchy we've been thrown into. That makes us defensive, insecure, power-hungry, approval-seeking, and afraid of being wrong.

Here's how it shows up at work:

- **Ego** makes us talk over others, ignore input, or defend bad ideas just because they're ours.

- **Fear** keeps us from taking risks, telling the truth, or challenging the status quo.

- **Lack of empathy** makes us terrible collaborators. We assume people think like we do, or worse, that they *should*.

- **Control issues** lead to micromanaging, overloading yourself, and burning out.

- **Avoidance** leads to resentment, drama, and slow-motion failure.

Sound familiar? It should. You've seen this. You've *been* this. Because again, *we all suck*. That's the baseline.

Leadership Starts in the Mirror

One of the hardest truths you'll read in this book is this: *If you're constantly surrounded by dysfunction, you're not just witnessing it, you're part of it.*

That's not shame. That knowledge is power.

Because once you accept that *you* are part of the problem, you become capable of being part of the solution. You can evolve. You can change how you lead, how you respond, how you build. You can stop adding noise and start creating clarity.

But only if you're willing to look inward first. Because the real work? It starts with three words: *"Am I contributing?"*

No System Fixes a Sick Culture

You can have the perfect strategy, tools, software, and organization chart, and it still may not matter.

If the people inside the machine aren't aligned, if they don't feel seen, heard, trusted, or empowered, it breaks, every time. Dysfunction doesn't happen because of one bad hire. It happens because the system tolerates, or even rewards, the wrong behaviors. Now, ask yourself, who creates the system?

People.

Systems break when we ignore how people work, or more importantly, how they *don't*. Want to build a better business? You have to get good at dealing with the mess in the middle: the egos, emotions, miscommunications, and power dynamics that derail everything.

The Good News

People may suck, but we don't have to stay that way.

This book will walk you through how to stop sucking, at leadership, communication, collaboration, and being a decent person in a business setting. It starts here, in the mud, with a brutally honest look at how easy it is to cause problems, even when you think you're doing everything right.

If you're willing to own your part, you can change everything.

Culture. Performance. Relationships. Results.

It just starts with understanding three words:

People. Fucking. Suck.

CHAPTER 2: AM I THE DRAMA?

This is really not only the million dollar question, but also the million-dollar realization. The moment you ask this question, *and actually mean it*, you're instantly ahead of most people in your organization.

People will rarely look at themselves. They're too busy pointing fingers, rewriting history, or telling stories about how everyone else just doesn't get it. The leaders who grow, and become the inspiration for others, are the ones who learn to pause, take a breath, and ask:

"How am I contributing to this mess?"

Not "Am I to blame?"
Not "Is this all my fault?"
But: *"What role am I playing in the dysfunction?"*

Because you always play a role. Pretending otherwise is how things go from annoying to toxic.

Ego, Fear, and the Fantasy of "What If?"

Most dysfunction is fueled by ego and fear.

Your ego tells you that you're right. Fear tells you not to speak up, but to wait for the right moment that never comes. Ego makes you steamroll the conversation, in case someone else has a better idea. Fear makes you disappear.

Together, they create a fantasy world where everything could be better:

- *What if my boss communicated better...*

- *What if the team was more motivated...*

- *What if people weren't so sensitive...*

- *What if they'd listen to me...*

Here's the brutal truth: "What If" is the language of people who don't want to do the work.

Yes, sometimes your boss *does* suck, and sometimes your company *is* broken. But unless you're actively looking at *your* own patterns, your own behavior, your own impact, and your own blind spots, you're not fixing anything. You're just narrating the collapse.

A Lesson in Ego from a Dumbass 22-Year-Old

At 22, I was making $100 an hour as a consultant, and in 1996, that pretty much felt like C-level money. I'd been hired by the CEO of a financial services firm Herb Vest, who of course named his firm H.D. Vest Financial Services. I was basically told to "get shit done." So that's what I did.

On day one, I walked into the "Web" department. I found someone with the title "web coordinator" and said, "Great, you now work for me!"

That was the level of unchecked confidence I had. I didn't ask. I just declared. I had no title. No direct authority. I didn't give two shits about who her manager was, or what that person thought about me. I just had sheer determination and a hell of a lot of technical skill. Now granted, it did work, because I *was* good at what I did, but I was also walking around like a one-man wrecking crew.

I had zero awareness of how I was making people feel. I didn't think about the guy whose team I bulldozed. I didn't stop to ask how I was being perceived. I was too busy "winning."

Here's the thing: *you can get results and still be the problem.*

Just because the project gets delivered doesn't mean the culture's healthy. Just because you're right doesn't mean you're helping. Just because people tolerate your leadership doesn't mean they trust it.

Years later, I looked back on that moment and realized: I had a team… but I was still treating people like tools. Like levers to pull, not people to lead.

That works for a little while. Eventually, the wheels come off.

So… How Do You Know if You're the Problem?

Here are some clues:

- You think most problems would be solved if *other people* just changed.

- You've had the same conflict with different people at different companies.

- You're "busy" all the time but nothing important seems to change.

- You avoid conflict until it explodes.

- You believe you're the only one who really *gets it.*

Want to know what makes someone great to work with? It's not that they're perfect. It's that they're *reflective.*

They say things like:

- "Let me think about that."

- "You might be right."

- "That didn't land how I intended."

- "What do you need from me?"

- "How did I make that harder?"

That kind of self-awareness is a superpower. It builds trust. It lowers defenses. It makes people feel like they can actually tell you the truth without fearing retribution or a cold shoulder.

It's also *contagious*. When you model ownership, others follow.

From "Being Right" to Being Effective

Here's something that will piss off your ego:

Being right isn't enough. You have to be effective.

You can be the smartest person in the room and still suck to work with. You can have the best strategy and still get ignored. You can mean well and still be causing harm.

Leadership isn't about always being right. It's about creating an environment where *the right things can happen* consistently, clearly, and without drama.

That means creating *safety*. Emotional safety. Intellectual safety. Cultural safety. People need to feel like they can tell the truth, even when it's hard, without being punished for it.

That kind of culture doesn't magically appear. It starts with someone being willing to go first.

That someone is you.

Quick Gut Check: Are You the Drama?

Let's make it simple. Read each of these. Answer to yourself, honestly, then pause, and take a second look.

- I let people finish their thoughts, even when I think they're wrong.

- I don't need to be involved in every decision.

- I can admit when I'm wrong... without a 5-minute justification monologue.

- I ask for feedback regularly, and actually listen to it.

- I create space for disagreement without punishment.

- I don't have to win to feel valued.

If you're checking a few boxes? Great. You're doing the work. If not? That's okay. That's why we're here.

The Invitation

You don't have to be perfect. But you *do* have to be curious. You have to be willing to wonder, "What's my role in this?" before you fire off the next email or light up your team in a meeting.

The people who can ask that, and mean it, are the ones who actually change things. They build the cultures everyone else wishes they worked in.

And that starts by asking the simplest, but sometimes the hardest question in business:

Am I the drama?

CHAPTER 3: YOUR REALITY IS NOT THE REALITY

You live in your own POV, and so does everyone else. Until you understand that, empathy is impossible and leadership becomes theater.

Let's slow down for a second. You've probably read a few chapters now and are either nodding in agreement or mentally drafting a list of all the people in your life who "really need this book."

Here's the truth: *you need this chapter*. It's the one that everything else builds on. It's the part most people skip, and it's the reason most relationships, personal and professional, fall apart.

Let's talk about **Point of View**.

We Don't See the World as It Is

Our view of the world is not shaped by reality, but by who *we* are.

Every conversation you've ever had, every fight, every compliment, every slight, you've interpreted all of it through your own lens. That lens is built from your experiences, trauma, values, fears, childhood, culture, education, family, mentors, bullies, heartbreaks, and victories.

Your POV is not neutral.

It's not objective.
It's not even close.

It's *yours*, and that makes it incredibly powerful and dangerously limited.

Everyone Has Their Own Movie Playing

Picture this: You're sitting in a meeting, and you pitch an idea. Someone shoots it down without much thought. You feel dismissed, disrespected, and maybe even humiliated.

But what if...

- That person just got off the phone with their kid's school because their son was arrested for DUI.

- Their dog is in surgery and they haven't slept in 2 days.

- They're battling imposter syndrome, and your confidence triggered their insecurity.

- They're not even *hearing* you; they're just surviving the day.

Or... maybe they're just an ass, but most of the time, it's more complicated than that.

People are walking around with invisible weight. You don't see the grief, the anxiety, the stress, the fight they had that morning, the financial pressure, the chronic pain, the heartbreak, the shame.

You have no idea what's shaping someone else's POV in any given moment, just like they don't know what's shaping yours.

Your POV Isn't Static

Most people think their worldview is consistent. "I'm just like this." But the truth is, your POV *shifts constantly*. It's affected not just by your past, but by your present.

- You respond with anger at a coworker... but you're actually just raw from a divorce.

- You shut down in meetings... but it's not about the project, it's that you just lost a parent.

- You micromanage... because your confidence is shot after your kid told you they hate you.

These things *bleed*. They always do.

You bring your whole life to work, whether you mean to or not, and so does everyone else.

Why This Matters in Business (and in Life)

When we forget this, when we assume people see the world like we do, or "should" act a certain way, we destroy trust. We overreact and misread intent. We label people instead of learning from them.

We lose the opportunity to connect.

Empathy isn't soft. It's strategic. It's what lets you lead effectively, resolve conflict, retain talent, and stop wasting emotional energy on misinterpretations. It's what helps you stop making everything about *you*.

Pause and Think:

Before you react to someone, ask:

- What *might* they be carrying right now that I can't see?

- How might their history or stress be shaping this moment?

- What part of *my* POV is coloring this situation?

Then go a layer deeper:

- Why did *that* comment piss me off so much?

- Why did I take *that* tone?

- Am I reacting to what just happened, or something I've been carrying around for years?

The goal isn't to excuse bad behavior. The goal is to understand that people are far more complicated than whatever version you've created of them in your head.

The Leadership Lens

As a leader, this is non-negotiable. If you don't understand that people are operating from wildly different realities, you'll try to manage everyone the same, and you will fail.

Empathy gives you leverage. It gives you context, and it gives you the ability to navigate complex people without losing your mind or your team.

Final Thought

Your POV isn't wrong, but it's not universal. The sooner you realize that, the sooner you stop being confused, offended, or disappointed by the fact that people aren't wired just like you.

Because they're not. They never were, and they never will be.

That's not a flaw. That's the whole point.

Reflection: Check Your Lens

Take 10 minutes. Be honest. No one's reading this but you.

Think of a recent situation at work that frustrated you.

- What did *you* feel at that moment?

- What story did you immediately tell yourself about the other person?

- What assumptions were you making?

Now flip it.

- What *might* have been going on in *their* world that you didn't see?

- How could their past experiences or current stress have shaped their behavior?

What was your own POV that day?

- Were you tired? Distracted? Insecure? Angry about something unrelated?

- How might *your* state have colored the way you showed up?

If you could reframe the situation through a more empathetic lens, what would you do differently next time?

This isn't about letting people off the hook. It's about understanding what the hook actually is, and whether you're already hanging from it.

CHAPTER 4: FEAR AND EGO, THE TWIN ENGINES OF DYSFUNCTION

The invisible forces behind your worst decisions, and everyone else's too.

Let's talk about the two things that have quietly destroyed more teams, more projects, and more working relationships than any bad idea or bad hire ever could: **fear** and **ego**.

They don't come into the room loudly. They don't raise their hands in meetings. They don't show up on your calendar. But they're always lurking, in your hesitation to speak up, in your defensiveness when someone pushes back, in your need to be right, and in your fear of being found out.

They're the invisible hand guiding the drama, the burnout, the resentment. They're the reason that brilliant teams fall apart. They're why "culture" goes sour. They're why we start turning on each other, instead of turning toward each other.

Let's Start with Ego

Most people think ego looks like arrogance. Someone who's puffed up and loud. Someone flexing their title or showing off in every conversation. That's one version for sure, but ego is even sneakier than that.

Sometimes ego shows up as the inability to listen. It can be the need to control everything because no one else can do it "just right." Sometimes ego convinces you that you're being a good leader, when really, you're micromanaging people into silence because deep down, you're afraid they might outperform you.

Ego isn't about confidence. It's about *self-protection*. It's the armor you wear when you feel uncertain. It's the thing that says, *"If I look strong, no one will see that I'm actually afraid."*

The more successful you become, the harder your ego is to detect. That's because it starts dressing itself up in the clothes of "high standards," "strong opinions," or "decisive leadership." But make no mistake, if you can't sit down, shut up, and really listen to others when it counts, your ego is running the show.

True Leadership Is Ego-less

Here's the thing no one tells you when you're climbing the ladder. The higher up you go, the less it should be about *you*.

Real leadership means getting excited when someone else brings a better idea to the table, and not feeling threatened when the idea is not yours. It means being willing to hand off the mic, step out of the spotlight, and *truly* collaborate. It's about wanting to get to the *best* decision, not just the one that makes you look smart.

Sometimes that best decision lives in another department. Sometimes it comes from someone who has less experience. Sometimes it's a solution you never would've come up with in a million years.

If you can recognize it and say, "Yes, that's better," without needing to spin it back to yourself or claim the credit, then you're leading.

When ego is loud, leadership suffers. But when ego is quiet, when it's in check, you create space for real growth, better outcomes, and stronger teams.

Here's the hard truth: *What's best for you in the short term is rarely what's best for the company in the long term.* Taking credit, controlling every detail, protecting your turf may feel satisfying in the moment, but it's a short-lived success, a shallow win. It burns out your team, kills innovation, and isolates you faster than you think.

The leaders who last are the ones who understand this: *Legacy is built on shared success.* Shared success can only happen when your ego isn't taking up all the space in the room.

Then There's Fear

Fear is quieter, but it is everywhere.

It's in the person who never speaks up in meetings. It's the boss who avoids giving feedback because they don't want to be "too harsh." It's the senior leader who overworks themselves because if they slow down, someone might notice they're not perfect.

Fear is the thing whispering to you that you're not enough, that you're not safe. That if you show any vulnerability, you'll lose your authority. So instead, you play it safe, hide behind your title, or throw others under the bus. Anything to avoid that sense of exposure.

What's actually wild is how often fear and ego work together. Fear shows up, then ego rushes in to cover it up. You're afraid of looking weak, so your ego makes you rigid. You're afraid of being wrong, so your ego makes you dismissive. You're afraid of being irrelevant, so your ego needs to prove you're still the smartest person in the room.

Left unchecked, this combo poisons everything.

When Ego Cost Me a Great Hire

Years ago, I hired a guy who was one of the most talented

engineers I'd ever met. He was smart, fast, and insightful. The kind of person who not only solved problems, but made the entire team better just by being in the room, and I ruined it.

Not intentionally. I wasn't yelling, insulting him, or being overtly toxic, but I couldn't let go. I nitpicked and overexplained. I questioned decisions that didn't need questioning, all under the banner of "mentoring." The truth is, I didn't want him to outshine me. His brilliance made me feel replaceable.

Instead of addressing that feeling, the insecurity, I let my ego do the work, and it wrecked the relationship.

He left three months later, and he was right to.

That moment hit hard, because I wasn't "being a bad boss." I wasn't doing what most people would consider obviously wrong, but I was afraid. Afraid of being irrelevant, not being the best. Because I didn't deal with it, my ego poisoned something that could've been great.

Since then, I've done the work to recognize those patterns. It started by admitting that fear and ego were driving the bus, not leadership.

When You Lead From Fear, Everyone Feels It

If you're in a leadership role, and that includes team leads, founders, department heads, or just the most experienced person in the room, your fear doesn't stay with you. It spreads.

When you lead from fear, your team starts second-guessing themselves. When your ego dominates the room, people stop speaking up. When you get defensive in feedback conversations, no one brings up the real issues anymore.

Culture isn't created by handbooks or values posters. It's created by how leaders handle fear, their own and others'.

You want to create a culture that works? Then your people need to feel safe.

Safe to speak. Safe to fail. Safe to grow.

That only happens when *you* aren't being ruled by fear and ego yourself.

You Can't Lead What You Won't Own

You don't need to get rid of fear and ego completely, that's not realistic. Intrinsically they exist in us as survival instincts, but you do need to recognize when they're in the driver's seat.

You need to build the muscle that lets you *pause* when you feel threatened, instead of reacting. To ask yourself, "Is this really about them, or am I just afraid of something right now?" To lead anyway, even when you're unsure, without letting your ego compensate for your discomfort.

That's where trust is built and that's where real leadership thrives.

Reflection: Fear and Ego Check

Take 5 minutes. No judgment. Just honesty.

1. Where does fear show up in your work life? What are you most afraid people will think or see?

2. When does your ego show up? What are you trying to protect?

3. Have you ever lost a great teammate, opportunity, or moment because you couldn't admit you were afraid?

4. What's one area where you can show up with *less armor* and *more honesty* starting this week?

CHAPTER 5: SHUT UP AND LISTEN

Empathy is the superpower you're probably not using, and the one everyone around you wishes you would.

We don't need another training module on "soft skills." We need people who actually give a shit.

Not pretend to. Not act like it when it's convenient. People who genuinely try to understand what someone else is going through, even when it's messy, uncomfortable, or completely different from their own experience.

That's empathy, and it's not optional anymore. Empathy allows you to keep your job, instead of being replaced by the latest ChatGPT model.

If you want to be better at work, in leadership, in relationships, or just as a human being, you need to understand that **empathy is the foundation of all of it.**

Everyone Has Their Own POV, So What?

Back in Chapter 3, we talked about point of view. The idea that you see the world through your own lens, and so does everyone else. Your reactions, beliefs, and behaviors are all shaped by your past and your present.

Here's the next step: **If everyone has their own lens, then empathy is the only way to truly connect.**

Empathy says, *"I know I don't see what you see, but I'm willing to try."*

It's not about being right. It's not about fixing anyone. Sorry, Coldplay. It's about being present enough to say, "I see that this matters to you, and I care."

It changes everything.

What Empathy Actually Is (and Isn't)

Let's break it down, because this part really matters.

Empathy is not:

- Agreeing with someone to keep the peace.

- Nodding and smiling while secretly judging them.

- Saying, "I totally understand" when you really don't.

- Pity.

- Sympathy.

- A performance.

Empathy *is*:

- Slowing down and actually listening.

- Being curious instead of assuming.

- Asking better questions.

- Letting go of your need to control the narrative.

- Sitting with someone else's experience, even if it's wildly different from your own.

Empathy, by definition, is the ability to understand and share the feelings, thoughts, or experiences of another person, *as if you were in their position, without needing to agree or fix anything.*

It's looking at the person in front of you and saying, *"I might never fully get what you're going through, but I'm here, I'm listening, and I want to understand."*

Let's be clear, empathy is *not weakness.* It doesn't mean letting people walk all over you. It doesn't mean coddling, or enabling, or making excuses.

Empathy is strength. It's awareness. It's leadership, regardless of whether you have a title.

Yes, it's hard as hell because real empathy forces you to slow down, shut up, and set your ego aside.

Those Crazy Canucks!

When I took a leadership role at Ashley Madison, I moved to Toronto for the job. Now, this was after I'd spent years building and leading teams in Texas. I knew fast-paced. I knew high-pressure. I knew how to push hard, drive projects, and demand results.

What I didn't know, and what Canada taught me, was empathy at scale. For a moment, put aside any political thoughts that might be driven by your own POV. What I'm talking about here is being exposed to a different point of view than what I personally grew up with in Fort Worth, Texas.

I mean let's look at a simple example that almost every family deals with sooner or later: *maternity leave.*

In Canada, it is one year, *minimum.* There is no debate, and no guilt.

I asked a coworker once if they thought a year was reasonable for maternity leave. I was used to women taking eight weeks, sometimes even six! They looked at me and said, *"A year? No way. That baby needs their mother for longer than that. It's the most important part of their lives together."*

That hit me, because I realized how deeply my version of "normal" was shaped by an environment that rewarded burnout over balance.

Here's what I learned: Empathy isn't just something you do in a moment. It can be built into systems. It can show up in policy, in priorities, in the way people treat each other without even thinking about it.

In Canada, I saw a culture that didn't just say "we value people", it actually did. Meetings moved a little slower. People gave space to talk. There was a level of patience, of listening, that felt foreign at first. But damn, was it effective.

The funny part, besides the fact I was working for Ashley freaking Madison, the work still got done. Sometimes faster, sometimes more thorough, because people weren't operating from fear. They were operating from trust.

That experience changed the way I saw everything. Empathy wasn't a buzzword in Toronto, it was a way of operating, and it worked.

The Listening Crisis

Let's get honest for a second: *Does anyone actually fucking listen anymore?*

Most conversations aren't conversations. They're monologues with occasional pauses.

We listen just long enough to form a response. We interrupt, we assume, and then we jump in with "Yeah, but…" or "Well, in my experience…"

Then we wonder why people feel disconnected. Why no one opens up. Why is everyone always so guarded?

Because listening is rare, and being heard is even more rare.

If you want to understand someone, if you want to lead, collaborate, build trust, or even just have *less drama* in your life. You have to shut the fuck up long enough to hear what's actually being said.

The fool speaks while the wise person listens. That saying isn't famous because it sounds nice, it's famous because it's true. Be the one, this time, that chooses *wisely*.

Empathy Isn't Just for Leaders

You don't need a team, or a title, to practice empathy. You just need a brain, a heart, and the willingness to pause.

If you're on a team, empathy makes you a better coworker. If you're working with customers, it helps you solve their real problems, not just the ones they're yelling about. If you're burned out, empathy helps you give grace to the people around you instead of resenting them for things they're probably struggling with too.

The great thing is that *empathy is contagious.* When people feel understood, they show up differently.

They collaborate more.
They trust more.
They stay longer.
They give a shit.

All of that starts with *you*.

Reflection: Practice Empathy, For Real

Ask yourself:

1. Who have I talked over, dismissed, or misunderstood this week?

2. Where have I been more focused on being "right" than being understanding?

3. What's one moment this week where I can practice *actual* listening, without an agenda, and without focusing more on my reply, than what I am hearing.

You don't have to agree to care. You don't have to fix it to be present. If you want to be better, and if you want to be *heard*, you've got to learn to shut up and listen first.

CHAPTER 6: YOU ARE NOT THE MAIN CHARACTER

The company doesn't exist for you. It exists to survive, and you are either helping or hurting.

Let's break a myth that's been slowly poisoning the modern workplace:

Your company does not exist to make you happy.

It doesn't exist to validate your career goals.
It doesn't exist to give you meaning.
It doesn't even exist to take care of you, not really.

The company exists *to survive*, and if possible, to thrive. That's it.

It exists to make money for whomever owns it, whether that be a private company or a public company. It exists to deliver shareholder value, and if it stops making money, it dies. When something is trying to survive, it does what all living things do: it evolves, it grows, and if necessary, *it cuts off the parts that are holding it back.*

The Organism

I want you to picture a company like an *organism*. Not a machine. Not a structure. A living, breathing creature. Let's say it is similar to an octopus. Honestly, that's what it feels like most days.

You've got a head (leadership, strategy, finance), and a bunch of tentacles. Each one is doing something different.

Sales. Product. Support. Marketing. Engineering. HR. Customer Service. Fulfillment.

Each tentacle has to move with purpose, in coordination with the others, or the whole organism suffers. If one tentacle gets tangled, becomes bloated, slow, toxic, or non-functional, the organism suffers.

The head cuts it off.

Not because it's evil. Not because it's heartless. Because that's what organisms do when they're trying not to die.

True.com: When the Tentacles Took Over

I learned this the hard way at True.com, the first online dating site I worked for.

When I joined the company, we were growing like crazy. We had funding, momentum, and energy. We had a founder who had successfully built and sold another company. He wanted to build something *big* again.

So we did what a lot of startups do: we scaled fast. Too fast.

We didn't fully know what our key levers were, what departments were mission-critical and which were nice-to-haves. But we hired for all of them. At one point, we were sitting on *300+ employees* spread across dozens of departments. Everyone was working, everyone was busy, and honestly? A lot of it *felt* exciting.

But underneath the surface, the organism was bloated. We had too many tentacles, and they weren't working in sync. We didn't know which functions were actually feeding the business and which were just consuming energy.

We learned too late that our founder, while brilliant, had burned through *$55 million* of capital trying to figure that out. We probably could have built a thriving company on $10 million. But we were trying to do too much, too fast, without asking the hard questions.

So what happened?

We cut, hard. We laid off *two-thirds of the company.* Not because they weren't good people. Many were. Not because we didn't care. We absolutely did. But because if we didn't, *we were all going down with the ship.*

We had to survive. So we focused.

We looked at what was driving revenue, creating real value, and actually kept the lights on, then we reorganized everything around that. Within 60 days, we went from hemorrhaging cash to operating in the black.

The organism lived, and began to thrive.

But it only lived because we stopped treating everyone like they were equally essential and started acting in the best interest of the company's survival.

You Are a Cost

Here's the part no one likes to hear: If you work at a company, *any* company, **you are a cost.**

It doesn't matter how nice your boss is.
It doesn't matter how great the culture is.
It doesn't matter how long you've been there.

You cost money, and if you're not bringing in *more value* than you consume, then from a purely biological business perspective, you are weighing the organism down.

Let me be clear: That doesn't make you a bad person. It doesn't mean you don't matter. It means you're in a system, and systems only survive by being efficient.

So if you're not performing, or if your department isn't contributing to the organism's movement, strength, or growth... If your job is redundant, outdated, or under-leveraged...

You're at risk, and that's not personal. *That's math.*

But What About Benefits? Culture? Perks?

A lot of people hear this and think, *"So companies don't care at all?"*

No, smart companies care a lot. Not because it's their moral responsibility. They care because happy, supported, loyal employees make the organism stronger.

That's why great companies offer great benefits. That's why they focus on culture. That's why they promote wellness, learning, growth, and recognition.

They know that an organism with a healthy nervous system moves faster and lasts longer.

But make no mistake, all of those things: benefits, overtime, perks, team outings, 401(k) matches, they only exist because they serve the larger goal, performance and survival.

The moment you become a drain on the system, or the system evolves past your function, you're expendable.

That's not cold. That's the reality of nature. A company is nature wearing a hoodie and a badge on a cute lanyard.

So What Do You Do With This?

If you're reading this and thinking, *"Damn, this feels harsh,"* it's not meant to be. It's meant to be honest. Because with honesty comes clarity. With clarity comes the opportunity to *stop waiting to be taken care of and start becoming indispensable.*

Do you want job security?

Don't just show up.
Don't just blend in.
Don't just coast.

Find ways to move the organism forward. Make the tentacle you're a part of essential to the health of the whole. Understand the mission. Align with the mission. Create more than you consume.

That's how you stick around. That's how you grow. That's how you thrive.

Reflection: Are You Helping the Organism Thrive?

Ask yourself:

1. How does the work I do every day connect to the success of the company?

2. Am I creating more value than I'm consuming?

3. If my role disappeared tomorrow, what impact would it have on the business?

4. How can I evolve *with* the organism instead of waiting for it to evolve past me?

You are not the main character. You are a critical piece of something bigger. That's not a demotion, it's a powerful invitation.

To matter.
To contribute.
To move in sync with something alive.

CHAPTER 7: WHY IS EVERYONE SO DIFFICULT?

Spoiler: They're not. You just expect them to behave like you.

Let's be honest, you probably ask yourself this question at least once a week:

"What is their problem?"

Coworkers who blow up over nothing. Managers who change direction mid-project. Team members who take everything personally. People who seem to go out of their way to make things harder.

It's exhausting. If you're not careful, it becomes your story about work: "This place is full of idiots! Am I the only person here who gets it?"

Here's the truth no one wants to admit: Most people aren't trying to be difficult. They're just not operating from your point of view.

"Difficult" Is Just Another Way of Saying "Not Like Me"

When someone doesn't communicate like you do, they feel rude. When someone doesn't process problems like you do, they're unmotivated. When someone doesn't react the way you would, they're wrong.

We don't say it out loud, but that's what's happening. We confuse being *different* with being *difficult*. We project our standards onto people who have completely different life experiences, communication styles, and stressors. Then we get upset when they don't react the way we think they should.

It's not that they're broken. They're just not you.

Behavior Is the Tip of the Iceberg

People show you *what* they're doing. They almost never show you *why* they're doing it.

It's like watching a storm roll in and assuming you understand the climate. You don't. You're just seeing the weather that day.

Someone being short with you could be carrying the weight of a sick parent. Someone missing a deadline might be trying to manage anxiety no one sees. Someone not participating in meetings might be battling burnout, imposter syndrome, or a lack of psychological safety.

You are interacting with the tip of a deeply personal, mostly invisible iceberg.

Yet, because we're human, we rush to fill in the blanks with whatever story matches our mood that day:

"They don't respect me."
"They're trying to sabotage me."
"They're being unprofessional."

Sometimes, yes, people are just being assholes. More often, they're reacting to their own fears, insecurities, or blind spots, just like you do.

The question is: can you see past the moment? Can you resist jumping to conclusions and instead get curious?

Stop Taking It So Personally

If I could staple one piece of advice to every desk in the world, it would be this:

"It's not about you."

We take everything so personally. We interpret every shift in tone, every change in plans, every missed invitation to a meeting as some kind of message, and then our ego rushes in to decode it.

"They must be mad at me."
"I'm being pushed out."
"This was targeted."

You don't need to dig for pain where none exists. *You don't need to make yourself the main character in someone else's Tuesday.*

Sometimes things just happen. Sometimes your coworker was snippy because they were late picking up their kid. Sometimes your boss didn't respond to your proposal because they were buried under their own firestorm of meetings and stress.

Sometimes it's not deep. It just is.

Yet we let these moments rot. We loop them in our heads and overanalyze. We create entire narratives from a three-word email or a side glance in a meeting.

Our brains are wired to detect threats, and in the absence of real danger, we create emotional ones. That's fear. That's ego. That's our insecurity looking for a place to land.

The Stories We Carry

I can't tell you how many times an employee has come to me carrying a burden they never needed to carry.

They were convinced that a canceled project, a change in direction, a decision made in some meeting above their pay grade, were targeted moves against them. That we were "phasing them out" or "ignoring their contributions" or "sending a message."

I remember one conversation in particular. An employee came to me, clearly nervous, and said, "I just need to ask... did I do something wrong?"

I was caught off guard, because I literally had *no idea* what they were talking about.

Turns out, I had made a change to team assignments. One which I felt was a minor adjustment. They weren't removed. They weren't demoted. They were just reassigned based on workload. But from their POV? It was personal. It meant something.

What followed was a 10-minute conversation. I explained the reasoning, the strategy, and how they were a key part of the plan. Just like that, their whole demeanor changed. They smiled, and relaxed. The fear had been named and dismantled.

So many of these moments are like that. People just want to know they're not being singled out. They want to know that they still matter, and the truth is, they do.

But the story in their head was drowning out the reality.

That's the thing about all of us. We all want to believe that everything is about us, especially the bad stuff. It's your ego's way of staying in control. But if you can let that go? Work gets easier. People get a lot less "difficult."

You are Someone Else's "Difficult Person."

We're so quick to label others, but here's the uncomfortable truth: *You're the crazy one to somebody else.*

You're the cold one, or the intense one. The one who doesn't communicate clearly. The one they're afraid to talk to.

Let that sink in for a second.

You've triggered someone's insecurities. You've misunderstood someone's intention. You've written that one-line email that sent someone spiraling.

We all have.

So maybe it's time to give a little more grace, to others, and to yourself.

What to Do Instead of Taking the Bait

Next time someone comes across as difficult, try this:

- **Pause before reacting.** Ask: "What might be going on here that I don't see?"

- **Assume it's not about you.** Seriously. Try that for one week and watch how your mental load drops.

- **Ask questions.** Instead of assuming, say, "Hey, I noticed you seemed frustrated. Want to talk about it?"

- **Tell the truth.** If *you're* the one taking something personally, speak up. Clear it out instead of letting it fester.

Remember that empathy doesn't mean excusing bad behavior. It means being curious before you get defensive.

Reflection: Difficult People and Difficult Stories

1. Who's the person at work I've labeled as "difficult"?

2. What story am I telling myself about them?

3. What might actually be going on beneath the surface?

4. Where am I taking something personally that might not be about me at all?

You don't have to like everyone. You don't have to agree with everyone. But if you can understand them, or at least accept that you don't understand them, you'll stop fighting battles that don't need to be fought.

That might be the most peaceful, productive shift you make in your career.

CHAPTER 8: IT'S USUALLY NOT THAT DEEP

The art of knowing when to let it go… and when to dig the hell in.

By now, you've probably realized something about working with people: it's never just about the project.

There are emotions, assumptions, histories, egos, insecurities, and stress. On top of all that, there's actual work to get done.

Sometimes, things feel off. Someone's behavior triggers something in you. A comment lands weird. A decision gets made and you're left wondering, "Was that about me?"

Welcome to the human side of business.

Here's where most people get stuck: they either overanalyze everything or ignore everything. They either make drama out of shadows, or pretend the smoke isn't there when the fire is already spreading.

Emotional maturity is knowing the difference.

This chapter is about building that muscle, the ability to pause, assess, and decide: *Is this something to let go, or something to dig into?* Because the truth is, both responses are necessary. You just need to know when to use which.

The Pendulum of Overthinking and Under-Caring

People tend to swing between extremes:

Some people obsess over every little interaction, tone, or email. Others shut down entirely and decide nothing matters at all.

The first leads to anxiety. The second leads to apathy. Both lead to burnout. The magic is in the middle.

Maturity is knowing the difference:

- When it's not that deep, *let it go.*

- When it is that deep, *dig in.*

This chapter is about learning the difference. And why it matters more than almost anything else in your career.

When It's Not That Deep

You weren't invited to a meeting. It's not a conspiracy. Your manager seemed cold today. Maybe they're just tired. A coworker gave short answers in an email. They might just be hyper-focused, or human.

You do not need to investigate every awkward moment like it's a crime scene. You don't need to create a Netflix-level backstory for every short email.

Sometimes it's just not that deep. If you're going to survive working with other people, you need to build the muscle that lets you pause, breathe, and say:

"Maybe they're just having a day."

Quick Gut Check:

- Is this a pattern or a one-off?

- Do I have all the facts?

- Would it help to ask, or will time sort it out?

Learning to stop taking everything personally is a superpower.

When It Is That Deep

But sometimes... It is that deep.

The thing is, you probably already know when it is. Because the signs are usually there. You just have to be willing to listen.

You had a rough performance review. Your manager keeps asking for something different than what you're delivering. You're missing deadlines, or people have continually stopped including you in important conversations.

That's not random. That's smoke.

If you don't open your ears, tune in, and investigate? That smoke turns into a fire, the kind that burns up your credibility, your relationships, and your opportunities.

People rarely get blindsided when they're paying attention. The clues are usually there. You just have to stop telling yourself they're not a big deal.

Don't wait for someone to spell it out in bold red letters. If you're hearing consistent feedback, or seeing consistent outcomes, it's time to dig in.

Empathy doesn't mean silence. Self-awareness doesn't mean self-abandonment.

Sometimes the most empathetic thing you can do for yourself and your team is face the issue head-on.

The Only Way Out Is Through

When something *is* that deep, avoiding it won't make it better.

Here's what usually happens instead:

- You say nothing to keep the peace.

- The resentment builds.

- You vent to a few trusted coworkers.

- The dynamic gets worse.

- Eventually, you blow up or burn out, or both.

The person causing the problem? They're confused, because you never said anything.

If something feels off, if it feels *heavy*, and that feeling lingers for more than a few days, you owe it to yourself (and your team) to deal with it.

This doesn't mean confrontation. It means conversation. It means honesty. It means asking questions and being willing to name what others won't.

Hard conversations are never fun, but they're almost always worth it.

The Smoke You Ignore Is Usually Fire

Years ago, I had a guy on my team at Reflex Media. A product lead. He was smart, charismatic, fast-moving, and people liked him. He said all the right things. He *started* strong.

For a while, I thought we were really doing well. Projects were in motion. The team had direction. He was basically the "golden boy." The guy who seemed like he really *got it*.

But then, there was smoke. People started telling me things, subtle things.

"Something feels off."
"We're not finishing what we start."
"He's making promises he can't keep."

I wanted to believe it wasn't a problem. I *needed* to believe it wasn't. We were *almost* getting shit done. Part of me thought, let's not rock the boat.

I even said to the founder: "We have a problem... I just don't know how bad it is yet."

Then I didn't dig. I didn't push. I told myself it would pass. That it wasn't that big of a deal. That was my mistake.

Because it *was* that deep. The fire that had been quietly building turned into an inferno. It cost us time, money, trust, momentum, all of it.

The full story? We'll get to that, but the lesson is this: When something feels off, and you keep hearing whispers, listen.

Smoke is usually fire. And the longer you wait, the harder it is to contain.

The Emotional Maturity Checklist

Want to know if you're doing the work? Read these slowly. If any of them make you twitch, that's probably your area to grow.

- I can let go of small stuff without spiraling.

- I know how to check my ego before jumping to conclusions.

- I don't avoid real problems just to keep the peace.

- I know when my feelings are valid, and when they're just fear.

- I can sit in discomfort without needing to fix it right away.

- I ask honest questions instead of telling false stories.

This is what it means to grow up at work. This is how you become someone worth following.

Wrapping Up Part 1: The Mirror Doesn't Lie

You made it through the hard part. You've looked inward. Faced the mess. Held up the mirror, and (hopefully) didn't throw it across the room.

You've owned your ego and recognized your patterns. You've started asking the right questions, and realizing that the problem isn't always "them."

That's rare, and it's powerful.

Part 1 was about reflection and brutal honesty.
It was about burning down the old stories and getting clear on what's really going on.

Part 2 is where we build.
It's where we take all this awareness and turn it into actual change. Because knowing better is useless unless you're willing to do better.

Finally: Burn the Bullshit

Grab a piece of paper, a fresh doc, or your Notes app.

Write down one story you've been carrying at work:

- A grudge.

- A belief about yourself.

- A narrative about someone else.

- Something you've decided "just is the way it is."

Now ask yourself:

- Is this actually helping me?

- Is this even true?

- Am I willing to let this go, or do I need to go deeper?

The work doesn't end here, but you've done the hardest part:

You stopped blaming everyone else, and started owning your part.

Now let's move forward, together.

CHAPTER 9: EMOTIONAL INTELLIGENCE IS NOT OPTIONAL

The skill that changes everything, and why most people still don't get it.

Let's start with a brutal truth: You can be brilliant. You can be hardworking. You can have experience, credentials, charm, talent, and ideas that would impress a room full of TED Talk alumni...

...and still completely fail at work because you can't read the room, take feedback, or manage your emotions.

That's Emotional Intelligence (EQ), and it's not optional anymore.

People love to throw the term around like it's a buzzword, but emotional intelligence isn't some fluffy leadership add-on. It's the core of everything: culture, collaboration, performance, longevity, retention, and most importantly, trust.

You want to be a leader? You want to work on a high-functioning team? You want to *not* make your coworkers' lives harder every day?

This is where you start.

What Emotional Intelligence Actually Is

IQ (Intelligence Quotient) measures how well you solve problems, use logic, and grasp complex ideas.

EQ (Emotional Intelligence) is your ability to recognize, understand, and manage emotions, in yourself and others.

Think of it like this:

- **IQ** gets you hired.

- **EQ** gets you promoted.

- **Low EQ** gets you fired.

Psychologist Daniel Goleman defined five key components of emotional intelligence. These are the building blocks that determine whether you're going to be someone who elevates a team, or someone who wrecks one.

Let's break them down.

Self-Awareness

The ability to recognize your own emotions, triggers, and impact on others.

This is the foundation. If you don't understand yourself, you can't manage yourself. You also sure as shit can't lead anyone else.

Signs of poor self-awareness:

- You say you're "just being honest," but constantly hurt people.

- You blame others for how you feel.

- You interrupt, dominate, or shut down in conversations, and don't notice.

- You take everything personally but never ask why.

- You can't receive feedback without spiraling.

People with low self-awareness don't realize when they're the common denominator in conflict. They also confuse *intent* with *impact*, and wonder why people react poorly when they are "just trying to help."

High self-awareness creates calm.
It's the ability to recognize: *"I'm triggered right now. Let me pause."* It's knowing how your tone affects a room. It's recognizing that your bad mood is about your broken water heater, not your teammate's email message.

High self-awareness is the foundation of all growth. If you can't name what's happening inside you, you'll never be able to manage it, and you'll keep creating chaos without even realizing it.

Self-Regulation

The ability to manage your emotions and respond rather than react.

It doesn't mean pretending not to feel things. It means not letting your emotions run the show.

It means:

- Not snapping at your team when you're frustrated.

- Not sending the angry email.

- Not making decisions just to "show them."

It's the pause between the feeling and the reaction.

Signs of poor self-regulation:

- You snap when under pressure.

- You ghost people or shut down when uncomfortable.

- You say things like, "I'm just a passionate person," to justify bad behavior.

- You fire off emails at 10 p.m. in all caps.

- You use stress as an excuse for cruelty or chaos.

People with low self-regulation create volatile work environments. You never know which version of them is going to show up.

Strong self-regulation means you can be trusted under pressure.

It's how you build trust. People follow leaders who are consistent, not emotionally volatile. Peers respect coworkers who stay composed under pressure. If you can't manage yourself, no one will trust you to manage a project, a team, or a crisis.

Motivation

Motivation in the EQ sense means being driven by internal values and purpose, not just status, titles, or rewards.

It means you show up and push forward because the work matters. Because progress matters. You care about doing a good job, even when no one's watching.

Signs of low motivation:

- You only work hard when someone's paying attention.

- You need constant praise to stay engaged.

- You blame others for lack of progress.

- You drop off the map when a project gets hard or boring.

Low-EQ individuals often blame others for their lack of drive: "This place doesn't inspire me." "My manager doesn't motivate me." High-EQ people know how to tap into their own reasons for showing up, and they use that to push through obstacles and setbacks.

This internal drive is what separates the people who quit when it's hard from the people who find a way.

As a leader, *motivation without drama* is one of the most attractive and trustworthy traits you can bring to the table.

Empathy

Empathy is the ability to understand and share the feelings of another, without needing to fix, judge, or insert your own experience.

We covered this deeply in Chapter 5, but it's worth repeating:

It means you:

- Actually listen when someone's speaking.

- Try to understand their perspective, even if you don't agree.

- Care about how your actions make other people feel.

Signs of low empathy:

- You cut people off or talk over them.

- You dismiss other people's stress as weakness.

- You make jokes when someone is being vulnerable.

- You assume people should "just get over it."

- You dismiss concerns as whining or weakness.

People with low empathy struggle to build trust. They miss social cues. They bulldoze conversations. They make people feel small, even when they don't mean to.

Empathy builds loyalty. It creates psychological safety. It's not about coddling. It's about understanding. Without it, leadership becomes control, not connection.

Social Skills

The ability to build relationships, communicate clearly, and move through complex group dynamics.

This is where everything comes together.

Self-awareness + self-regulation + motivation + empathy = someone you actually want to work with.

This isn't about being the most charming person in the room. It's about:

- Communicating clearly.

- Handling conflict maturely.

- Building rapport with a range of people.

- Knowing when to step in and when to back off.

Signs of poor social skills:

- You talk way more than you listen.

- You dominate meetings, or disappear in them.

- You don't know how to have hard conversations.

- You blame people instead of problems.

- You can't give or receive feedback without getting weird.

Low EQ here often looks like poor boundaries, inconsistent communication, or an inability to read the energy of a team.

This is also where poor EQ shows up in the inability to take criticism. If you fall apart or get defensive every time someone gives you feedback, you're not just struggling with confidence, you're struggling with emotional intelligence.

High-EQ individuals know how to stay open, adjust, and communicate in a way that builds trust, not drama.

Why EQ Is the Ultimate Power Move

Here's the truth: most people don't have high emotional intelligence. They've never been taught it. They've never practiced it and they don't think it's their job.

If you want to be effective, to lead, influence, grow, and make things happen, EQ isn't a nice-to-have. It's the whole damn game.

People with low EQ:

- Struggle to keep jobs long term.

- Can't maintain healthy work relationships.

- Don't take feedback well.

- Overreact to criticism.

- Underestimate the power of communication.

- Make everything personal, or nothing personal at all.

People with high EQ:

- Get promoted faster.

- Navigate conflict with ease.

- Are trusted during change.

- Are asked to lead, even without the title.

- Get things done without setting everything on fire.

The best part? *EQ can be learned.* You're not stuck where you are. It's not a personality trait. It's a skillset. The more you practice, the more natural it becomes.

This is the one skill, more than any other, that I wish future me could have taught to myself in my 20s. As I was walking around being cocky and thinking only of myself, I was pissing people off. Don't get me wrong, I was a good leader even then. What I didn't understand was what I could have accomplished with a full team, not just with skill alone, but with skill and a high EQ.

Reflection: Where's Your EQ Weak Spot?

Take inventory:

- Where do you lose control?

- Where do you shut down?

- Where do people pull back from you?

- Where are your blind spots?

Don't try to fix everything at once. Pick one area. Get curious and ask for feedback. Pay attention.

Emotional intelligence is the unfair advantage most people ignore, but not you. Not anymore.

Let's build it, one skill, one pause, one deep breath at a time.

CHAPTER 10: ACCOUNTABILITY SUCKS (UNTIL IT DOESN'T)

Why the thing you're avoiding is the thing that will set you free.

Let's get one thing out of the way: *Nobody likes being called out.*

Nobody wakes up thinking, "God, I hope someone gives me brutally honest feedback today that makes me question my entire existence!" Most people, even good people, will flinch when they're told, *"Hey, you dropped the ball."*

That's human. That's your ego. That's fear. If you want to grow, and lead, you've got to understand this.

Accountability is not punishment. It's power.

It's the thing that separates drama-prone, low-EQ chaos from high-trust, high-functioning teams. It's how you move from blaming others... to changing the game.

So yes, accountability sucks, but only until you realize it's the thing that will set you free.

What People Think Accountability Means

When people hear the word "accountability," they usually

picture some kind of punishment:

- The boss calls them into their office.

- A performance review filled with red flags.

- Being publicly thrown under the bus in a meeting.

- A micromanager breathing down their neck.

To be fair, that's how a lot of companies handle it. Badly.

In low-trust environments, "accountability" becomes a weapon. It's a way to shame and to blame people. To keep people afraid and compliant. Because of this, people learn to fear it, avoid it, and dodge it at all costs.

Real accountability? It's not about fear. It's not about blame. *It's about ownership.*

It's about raising your hand and saying, "This is mine. I own it," the good, the bad, and the ugly.

Guess what? People who can do that, they become unstoppable.

Signs You (Or Your Team) Avoid Accountability

You might think, "I'm pretty good at accountability," but are you, really?

Let's do a quick quiz:

- Do you cringe when someone gives you feedback, even when they're right?

- Do you start your explanations with "Well, the thing is..." instead of "You're right, that's on me"?

- Do deadlines slip without any follow-up conversation?

- Does the team know *exactly* who owns what?

- Or is it a murky mess of "We all kind of do that"?

When accountability is missing, here's what you'll see:

- Projects stall because no one really owns the outcome.

- Problems repeat themselves, because no one really investigates what went wrong.

- People start finger-pointing or playing the victim card.

- Feedback gets twisted into personal attacks.

- Trust erodes... fast.

A lack of accountability is like carbon monoxide: invisible, toxic, and eventually deadly.

Accountability Starts With You

Here's a truth that stings a little: *you can't hold others accountable if you're not holding yourself accountable first.*

That's leadership 101. That's adulting 101.

People don't follow your words. They follow your example.

If you dodge blame, they will too. If you get defensive when challenged, so will they. If you never admit when you're wrong, they'll learn to hide their mistakes too.

But when you show up and say:

"That's on me. I'll fix it." When you say that, you create space for others to do the same. This is the same whether you are leading a team or simply part of one.

This is where emotional intelligence comes back in.

People with *low* EQ take everything personally. They hear feedback and translate it as an attack on their identity. They twist "This could have been better" into "You're a failure."

So they deflect. They get defensive. They shut down.

But people with *high* EQ?

They understand that feedback isn't an indictment. It's information.

They can sit with it and process it, then decide what to do with it, without spiraling.

This is one of the most important leadership muscles you can build.

The Freedom of Ownership

Here's the wild part: the thing you're avoiding? The thing that feels heavy, scary, and uncomfortable?

It's the thing that gives you freedom.

Because the moment you say, *"This is mine,"* you stop waiting. You stop blaming. You stop being a victim of circumstance.

You start leading.

People trust you more when you take responsibility, not just for your successes, but for your stumbles. There's something magnetic about someone who can say:

"Yeah, I got that wrong. Here's what I'm doing about it."

It's not a weakness. It's credibility.

Owning your impact, especially when things go sideways, doesn't make people think less of you. It makes them respect you more.

It builds trust, culture, and it builds momentum.

Holding Others Accountable Without Becoming a Tyrant

Accountability doesn't have to be harsh. It just has to be clear.

People don't fail because they're evil. They fail because expectations were vague, follow-through was missing, or feedback came too late.

So if you're leading, formally or informally, here's how to build a culture of ownership:

- **Set clear expectations.** Ambiguity is the enemy of accountability.

- **Give feedback early and often.** Don't wait until it's "bad enough" to say something.

- **Separate the person from the behavior.** You're not calling someone *bad*. You're addressing a choice.

- **Model it relentlessly.** Own your misses. Celebrate others who do the same.

People will rise to the level of clarity you provide, or sink to the level of confusion you tolerate.

When I Didn't Hold Someone Accountable, and Paid for It

There was a time, earlier in my career, when I saw the red flags.

A teammate wasn't following through. Promises were made, then quietly dropped. People started avoiding certain projects. Morale dipped.

I waited and told myself it wasn't that bad. That we'd figure it out. Maybe they just needed more time or support.

The truth? I didn't want to deal with it.

I didn't want the awkward conversation. I didn't want to be the "bad guy." I didn't want to mess with what looked like momentum.

So I avoided it, and you can guess what happened.

Things got worse. Deadlines slipped. Trust eroded. Other team members felt unsupported and frustrated, not just with him, but with me.

Eventually, I had to step in. By then, the damage was done.

That was a leadership failure, *my* failure. Not because I didn't see the problem, but because I didn't act on it.

Lesson learned: accountability delayed is accountability denied. The earlier you name it, the better the outcome, for everyone.

Final Reflection: Your Accountability Inventory

Let's do a quick check. Grab a notebook and be honest.

- Where are you dodging responsibility right now?

- Where are you blaming others instead of asking, "What could I have done differently?"

- Where are you letting someone else slide, because confronting it feels hard?

- What project, task, or relationship needs you to show up more fully?

Here's the big one:

What would happen if I owned this fully, openly, and without excuse?

You don't have to fix everything today, but you do have to *own* it. The second you take responsibility is the second you take your power back.

Accountability isn't punishment. It's leadership. Once you learn to carry it with confidence instead of fear, it stops being a burden.

It becomes your backbone.

Now let's talk about how to give and receive that accountability in a way that actually works, without wrecking your relationships or setting the office on fire.

CHAPTER 11: COMMUNICATION THAT DOESN'T SUCK

Start Adulting

Let's be real: most workplace problems aren't technical. They're human, and they often come down to one thing:

People not saying what they mean, when it matters, in a way others can actually hear.

We avoid. We hint. We blow up. We sugarcoat. We send long-winded messages when a 3-minute honest conversation would solve the problem.

Then we wonder why everything feels confusing, tense, or just plain exhausting.

Communication is supposed to connect people. When it's done poorly, it creates distance. It creates stories and assumptions. The longer we go without addressing something clearly, the bigger and messier it becomes.

This chapter is about fixing that.

We're going to talk about how to say what needs to be said, without drama, without deflection, and without sounding like an asshole. Whether you're delivering feedback, advocating for yourself, or asking for clarity, your ability to communicate like an adult will directly impact your relationships, your performance, and your peace of mind.

Say the Thing

This might be the single best piece of communication advice you'll ever get.

Say. The. Thing.

Don't hint. Don't dance around it. Don't send a vague follow-up email and hope they "get the message."

If something needs to be said, then say it clearly, directly, and calmly.

That doesn't mean be harsh. It doesn't mean ignoring context or tone, but it does mean being honest. Don't make people guess what you're trying to tell them.

We spend so much time and energy trying to "soften" messages that we end up saying nothing at all. We bury the point so deep it never actually lands.

Say the thing cleanly and kindly, but actually say it.

Example: "I'm frustrated because this is the third deadline we've missed on this project, and I need to understand what's going on so we can get back on track."

NOT: "Well, I guess it's hard for some people to stay on schedule…"

See the difference?

Don't Weaponize Clarity

Clarity is powerful, but when misused, it becomes cruelty disguised as "just being honest."

Good communication isn't about winning. It's not about making someone feel small so you feel big. It's definitely not about dropping "truth bombs" and walking away like a smug little grenade launcher.

Real communication is about connection.

That means paying attention to your delivery. Watching your tone. Reading the room. Being honest in a way that invites understanding, not defensiveness.

You're not just trying to be right. You're trying to be effective.

Because if your message doesn't land, it doesn't matter how "right" you were. No one can hear you over the sound of their own armor clanking on.

Own Your Words (and Your Triggers)

Communication is not just about what you say. It's about how you show up.

If you walk into a conversation ready to defend, blame, or dominate, it doesn't matter how carefully you've worded your script. People will feel the energy before they hear the words.

So before you even open your mouth, ask yourself:

- Am I trying to connect or control?

- Am I here to understand or to be validated?

- Am I leading with curiosity or assumption?

Also, be real about your triggers. If someone disagrees with you and it sends you into a tailspin, that's something to unpack. If feedback feels like a personal attack every time, that's not a communication issue, that's an ego issue.

The more you understand your internal landscape, the less likely you are to hijack a conversation with emotion that doesn't belong there.

Timing Matters

You know this. You've felt this.

There's a moment when a conversation *can* happen, and a moment when it *shouldn't*.

Catching someone right after a stressful meeting? Probably not the time. Bringing something up in a group setting that deserves a private conversation? Poor judgment. Waiting three months to address something that happened in Week 1? You've missed your window.

Say the thing, but choose the moment.

Being emotionally intelligent means understanding context. It means recognizing when someone's walls are up and knowing that waiting one more day might actually help your message land.

Being urgent is not the same as being effective.

Communication Is a Two-Way Contract

Here's what no one teaches you: communication doesn't "work" unless both people are doing their part.

You can be clear, kind, thoughtful, and open, and someone still might not hear you.

You can ask great questions, and someone might still lie.

You can try your best, and the conversation still might crash.

That's not a reflection of your worth, but it *is* a reminder that you're only one part of the equation. Part of being a strong communicator is knowing when to stop over-functioning for people who aren't willing to meet you halfway.

Say the thing clearly, but recognize when your effort isn't being matched.

Communication Requires Practice

You don't get good at this overnight. You get good at it by practicing:

- Saying what you actually mean.

- Not reacting just because something feels uncomfortable.

- Sitting with silence instead of filling it with noise.

- Asking instead of assuming.

- Owning your part instead of blaming everyone else.

Every conversation is an opportunity to do it better. You'll screw up sometimes, and that's fine. But if you're willing to reflect, refine, and keep trying, you'll be miles ahead of most people who never even bother.

Final Thoughts

If you want to be seen as a leader, whether or not you have the title, start by speaking like one.

Speak clearly, respectfully, and honestly.

Say the thing, and say it like someone who actually gives a shit about being heard.

When it's your turn to listen? Do it with your whole attention. Communication isn't a performance. It's a relationship.

If you can get better at this, truly better, you'll be able to change your career, your relationships, and your day-to-day sanity.

Reflection: Say It Better Next Time

Take a moment to think through a recent conversation (or one you've been avoiding).

Ask yourself:

- What did I actually want to say?

- Did I say it clearly, or did I water it down?

- Was I trying to connect, or trying to win?

- How was my tone? My timing?

- What emotion was I bringing into the room, was it helpful?

- Did I listen, or just wait for my turn to talk?

- What would I do differently if I could hit replay?

Now think forward:

- What's one conversation I've been avoiding?

- What's the "thing" I need to say?

- What's holding me back?

- What could improve, for me and for them, if I said it well?

You don't need to be perfect. You just need to be willing to speak like the adult you're becoming.

CHAPTER 12: COLLABORATION WITHOUT LOSING YOUR MIND

(Or: How to Work With Other Humans Without Setting Your Laptop on Fire)

Let's get something straight: collaboration is not just "working together." It's navigating egos, communication gaps, unspoken agendas, unclear roles, half-baked ideas, and that one guy who always says "let's circle back" and then vanishes.

Collaboration is hard. But it's also non-negotiable.

No matter what role you're in, no matter how talented you are, you're going to have to work with other people. If you don't learn how to do that without going into fight-or-flight mode, your work will always suffer. Worse, you'll become someone nobody wants to collaborate with.

This chapter is about how to work with people, real people. People with quirks, baggage and different styles, in a way that makes the team stronger, not makes you resent life.

Teamwork Is a Skill (Not a Personality Trait)

Some people say, "I'm just not a team player." But here's the truth: that's not an identity. That's a skill gap.

Collaboration isn't about being extroverted. It's not about loving group work. It's about developing the ability to:

- Communicate clearly.

- Listen actively.

- Align goals.

- Share credit.

- Navigate conflict.

- Let go of control (when needed).

- Speak up (when it matters).

You don't have to be the loudest voice in the room. You *do* have to know how to be in the room, and contribute to something bigger than yourself.

If you want to grow, lead, or just not lose your mind at work, you need to treat collaboration like any other critical skill: practice it, get feedback, and get better.

The Real Reasons Collaboration Fails

People love to blame "poor communication" when teams fall apart. But let's go deeper. Collaboration breaks down when:

- **Roles are unclear.** Nobody knows who's doing what, and everything gets duplicated or dropped.

- **Ownership is fuzzy.** There's no single point of accountability, so no one makes decisions.

- **Egos get involved.** People want credit, control, or to prove a point, even if it hurts the project.

- **Assumptions go unchecked.** People don't clarify, ask, or check in, they just assume others "should know."

- **There's no trust.** People start working in silos or holding back because they don't feel safe being honest.

Most collaboration issues aren't about people being bad teammates. They're about systems being unclear, and emotions being unmanaged.

Fix the structure. Acknowledge the feelings. That's how you move forward.

Know Your Role, and Everyone Else's

One of the fastest ways to create team friction is role confusion.

Who's leading this? Who's the decision-maker? Who's responsible for delivery? Who's giving input vs. approving vs. just being kept in the loop?

If nobody answers these questions up front, collaboration turns into chaos. People overstep, disappear, get frustrated, or spin in circles waiting for someone else to act.

When starting a project, get clear on:

- Who owns the outcome.

- Who is providing input.

- Who needs to be informed.

- Who can give feedback, and when.

Clarity is kindness. And it keeps your team from slamming into each other like bumper cars.

Collaboration Without Codependency

Here's the trap: trying to make everyone happy.

You start over-accommodating. You delay decisions until there's consensus. You say yes when you mean no. You take on more work trying to be a team player.

That's not collaboration. That's codependence.

When we talk about codependence in the workplace, we're not talking about a clinical diagnosis. We're talking about behaviors that look like collaboration on the surface but are actually rooted in unhealthy dynamics.

Here's what that often looks like:

- You need constant reassurance from your teammates or boss before making decisions.

- You avoid conflict at all costs because you fear disrupting "the vibe."

- You start to tie your sense of worth or competence to how happy others seem with you.

- You take on more than your share of work to keep the peace or avoid confrontation.

- You feel responsible for other people's reactions, emotions, or performance.

In other words, you're no longer just working *with* people. You're becoming emotionally dependent on their approval, validation, or stability.

And what's worse? It *feels* like you're being a team player. You tell yourself, "I'm just being supportive," or "I don't want to be a burden," or "It's easier if I just do it myself." But really, you're slowly training your team to expect you to carry their emotional weight, and sometimes their actual workload too.

You become someone who's easy to take advantage of, even unintentionally. In the process, you burn out, grow resentful, or lose your voice entirely.

Real collaboration doesn't ask you to abandon your boundaries or pretend you're okay when you're not. It asks you to show up, fully, with your skills, your voice, and your limits.

Navigating Different Working Styles Without Losing Your Cool

One of the most underrated collaboration skills is the ability to work effectively with people who are nothing like you.

And let's be honest, that's hard.

You're detail-oriented. They're big-picture.
You love messaging. They want face-to-face.
You finish everything early. They sprint at the last minute.
You outline every step. They jump in and figure it out as they go.

If you're not careful, these differences turn into resentment:

"Why don't they just do it *my* way?"

Here's the truth: if everyone worked like you, your team would be painfully limited.

Diverse working styles are one of the biggest advantages a team can have, *if* you know how to navigate them. If not, they become landmines, misunderstandings, passive-aggressive comments, or side chats filled with frustration: "They just don't get it."

Collaboration isn't about forcing everyone to work the same way. It's about learning how to communicate across those differences. It's learning how to appreciate what someone else brings to the table, even if it's not how you would've done it.

Here's why this matters: If you can't work with people who are different from you, you will *never* build great teams. You will end up hiring people who mirror your strengths, reinforce your habits, and share your blind spots. That's not a team. That's an echo chamber.

Great teams are made up of tension, the healthy kind. The kind that happens when people challenge each other, stretch each other, bring different lenses and experiences and insights to the same problem. None of that works if the team can't *function* together.

That means you have to:

- Recognize your own working style, and stop expecting others to mirror it.

- Communicate your preferences clearly, instead of silently judging everyone who works differently.

- Ask how others like to work, and actually listen.

- Create systems that accommodate multiple approaches without lowering standards.

Let people know how to win with you. Ask them how to win with them. It's not about changing who you are, it's about creating space for all the parts of the octopus to move in sync.

If you only work well with people who are just like you, you're not collaborating. You're cloning, and that's not how you build anything great.

The Courage to Call It

Let's get real for a second: Not every collaboration works. Not every partnership can be fixed. Not every team dynamic is salvageable with one more coffee chat or communication workshop.

There comes a point where you have to say:

"We've tried. We've adjusted. We've communicated. It's still not working."

That doesn't make you a bad collaborator. It makes you a smart one.

The definition of insanity is doing the same thing over and over and expecting different results. In the workplace, a lot of us do exactly that. We keep hoping that next week's meeting will magically be different, or that this time they'll finally follow through, or that one more polite nudge will turn the tide.

Collaboration isn't just about effort. It's about fit.

So when is it time to "call it"?

Here are the signs:

- You've had multiple clear, respectful conversations and nothing changes.

- The dynamic is draining your team's energy and impacting performance.

- You're doing double the work just to manage the partnership.

- The emotional tax is outweighing the business value.

- You've tried new approaches, and the pattern repeats anyway.

It's okay to say: "This isn't working, and it's not personal."

But don't wait until you're at a breaking point. The earlier you bring it up, the easier it is to solve, or shift.

Here's how to bring it up like an adult:

1. **Stick to facts and patterns, not personal attacks.**
   "Over the last 3 projects, we've missed key deadlines because we weren't aligned on ownership."

2. **Name the impact.**
   "I'm finding that I'm spending more time double-checking and redoing work, which slows us both down."

3. **Be honest about your needs.**
   "I think we need to rethink how we're collaborating, or maybe even reassign roles to better match how we work."

4. **Leave room for a reset.**
   "I'm open to solutions, but we can't keep doing it this way."

You're not throwing someone under the bus. You're keeping the project, and your sanity, on track.

Sometimes the solution is simple. Shift roles, or add structure. Use a mediator. Sometimes the solution is separation, moving to different parts of the project, different partners, different teams. That's not failure. That's evolution.

The best collaborators aren't the ones who force harmony at all costs. They're the ones who know when to let go, pivot, and keep moving forward.

When It Works, It's Magic

You've probably been on at least one team where everything just *clicked*.

For me, that was during my time at H.D. Vest Financial Services. We were building one of the first online tax preparation platforms. We were a small but scrappy group, thrown into a challenge that, looking back, was a little insane: build a platform that could handle any federal tax return, and eventually dozens of state returns, from scratch, online, in just a handful of months.

We had no clue what we were doing at first. *None.* We had determination, and more importantly, we had *each other*.

We weren't perfect. There were cots in the back room because we worked late into the night. People cried from exhaustion. We lived off Mountain Dew and adrenaline. But what we had, in spades, was clarity, trust, and shared commitment.

No one was too good to take out the trash. Everyone carried their weight, and egos? They didn't have time to take up space, we had a tax season to meet.

We weren't collaborating because someone gave us training or said the word in a meeting. We were collaborating because we knew that if one piece fell out of sync, the whole thing could crumble.

And we did it.

We launched the site on time. We handled returns across the country. We scaled to a 60-person team the next year. To this day, people who worked on that project still say it was the best, most meaningful work of their careers. They also are still some of my best friends in the world.

That's not luck. That's what happens when collaboration is real, not just a buzzword. When people believe in the mission, respect each other, and pull in the same direction, magic happens.

Final Reflection: What Kind of Collaborator Are You?

Take a minute. Ask yourself:

- Do I clearly communicate what I need and expect?

- Do I know how to give input without taking over?

- Do I make space for others, or dominate the conversation?

- Do I clarify roles... or just hope people figure it out?

- Do I handle conflict, or avoid it?

Collaboration doesn't just happen. It's built.

Start building better. The people around you will thank you. Your future self will too.

CHAPTER 13: BOUNDARIES, BURNOUT, AND KNOWING WHEN TO SAY NO

If you don't set boundaries, your body will do it for you, usually by crashing.

Let's just say the quiet part out loud: Work will take everything you give it. Your messages will never stop pinging. There will always be one more thing. If you're good at your job? Even more will be asked of you.

Which means, if you don't draw the line, no one else will.

This chapter is about the invisible edge, the place where your sense of responsibility starts turning into resentment. Where helping turns into overfunctioning. Where passion turns into burnout. Where saying "yes" starts costing more than it's worth.

If you want to stay in the game, not just for the next sprint, but for the long haul, you're going to need boundaries, real boundaries. Ones you enforce. Ones that protect your energy, your focus, your sanity, and your actual life outside of work.

Let's talk about how to set them, and why it matters more than you think.

What the Hell Are Boundaries, Really?

Boundaries aren't walls. They're not ultimatums. They're not tantrums. They're definitely not a luxury reserved for people with more time or power.

Boundaries are clarity.

They're how you teach people to treat you. They're how you protect the energy you need to show up well, not just for others, but for yourself.

At work, boundaries sound like:

- "I'm offline after 6pm. Let's tackle this in the morning."

- "That's not my area, but I'll connect you with the right person."

- "I need uninterrupted time to finish this, can we check in after lunch?"

- "I'd love to help, but I don't have capacity for that right now."

It's not about being difficult. It's about being *sustainable*.

If you keep saying yes to everything, eventually you stop being good at anything, including your actual job.

Why Burnout Isn't a Badge of Honor

Somewhere along the way, we made exhaustion a personality trait.

"I'm so slammed."
"I haven't taken a real break in months."
"I was answering emails at midnight."

This gets said with weird pride, like being burned out makes you valuable. It doesn't. It makes you replaceable.

Burnout isn't just about feeling tired. It's a physiological and psychological response to prolonged stress with no relief. When it hits, it doesn't show up with a big warning sign. It creeps in.

You stop sleeping well. You feel constantly overwhelmed. Your productivity nosedives, and you start to resent the very work you used to love.

Worst of all? You disconnect from your team, your purpose, and yourself.

Burnout doesn't just dull your edge, it warps your thinking. You lose patience. You lose clarity. You stop being creative. You start making reactive, sloppy decisions that cost your team time, money, and trust.

The worst part? You don't even realize it. You're too deep in the grind to see how much you've changed.

Burnout isn't a rite of passage. It's a warning sign. Boundaries are the cure.

They're not selfish. They're not weak. Boundaries are the only way to ensure you can keep doing the work you care about, without losing yourself in the process.

Burnout doesn't just happen to "busy" people. It happens to people who care. People who give. People who say yes too much because they believe they should.

Setting boundaries is not a luxury. It's a necessity.

If you want to play the long game, you need to learn how to stay in the game.

That starts with protecting your most important asset: your energy.

Saying No Like an Adult

This is where most people stumble. They either avoid saying no altogether, or they swing to the other extreme and turn it into a fight.

Real boundaries don't require drama. They just require language.

Here are some ways to say no without burning bridges:

- "I'm not the best fit for this, but here's someone who might be."

- "I can't take this on right now, but let's revisit it next week."

- "I won't be able to help with that, but let me know how it goes."

- "I can do this, but I'll need to shift this other priority."

You don't owe anyone a dissertation. You don't need to overexplain. "No" is a full sentence. But if that feels too sharp, you can dress it up with context and kindness.

The goal is to say it clearly, not perfectly.

The Guilt Spiral, and How to Escape It

Every time we talk about boundaries, guilt shows up like it was invited.

"If I say no, they'll think I'm not a team player."
"If I take a day off, people will think I'm slacking."
"If I set limits, maybe I'm not as committed as I should be."

Let's get this straight:

- You can be committed and still say no.

- You can be dedicated and still need rest.

- You can be high-performing and still protect your peace.

Guilt is a liar. It will convince you that your worth is tied to your availability, but it's not. Your worth is in your value, and that value *plummets* when you're stretched too thin to think clearly.

You don't need to be everything to everyone. You just need to be effective, and that starts by managing your capacity like a pro, not a martyr.

Why Saying Yes All the Time Is Selfish (Yeah, We Said It)

Let's flip the script for a second.

You think you're being helpful. You think you're being the hero. You think by saying yes to everything, you're making life easier for everyone.

But if we're being honest?

Overcommitting isn't generosity. It's ego wrapped in martyrdom.

When you say yes to everything, even when you don't have the time, energy, or capacity, here's what actually happens:

- **You drop balls.** Deadlines slip. Quality suffers. People stop trusting you to follow through.

- **You create dependency.** People come to you instead of learning to solve problems themselves. You become a crutch, not a collaborator.

- **You breed resentment.** You say yes with a smile, but inside, you're pissed. Eventually, it leaks out in your tone, your texts, and your energy.

- **You steal opportunities.** By hogging all the work, even with good intentions, you may be robbing others of the chance to grow, contribute, or be recognized.

- **You become unreliable.** Not because you mean to, but because you've promised more than you can deliver. Now people are left holding the bag.

There's also a darker undercurrent here: when you say yes too much, it's often not about helping, it's about being needed. It's about feeling important. It's about trying to prove your worth by piling on more than you can carry.

That's not sustainable. And it's not fair to anyone, including you.

Here's the truth. If you always say yes, eventually someone else pays the price, whether it be your partner, your health, your work, your reputation, or your team.

So no, saying yes all the time isn't noble. It's unsustainable, and at its worst, it's selfish.

The most reliable, effective, respected people you know? They're not the ones saying yes to everything. They're the ones saying yes to the *right* things, and saying no with clarity and grace.

Boundaries aren't blocks. They're guardrails. They keep you aligned, focused, and steady.

Because the goal is not to do everything. The goal is to do the *important* things, with energy, excellence, and integrity.

Boundaries Make You Better at Your Job

Boundaries don't just make you healthier. They make you better.

When you manage your energy, time, and attention with intention, you make better decisions. You communicate more clearly. You get *more* done, and what you produce is higher quality.

Boundaries also set expectations with others. They reduce confusion. They give people clarity about what you will and won't do, and when.

You stop being the person who drops the ball. You start being the person who delivers with consistency and calm. You become known for your dependability, not your panic.

Now that's good for your career, because no one promotes the person who's constantly in chaos. They promote the person who shows up clear, consistent, and composed.

What Healthy Boundaries Actually Look Like

Let's paint a picture.

A person with strong boundaries:

- Has a clear understanding of what they can and can't take on.

- Communicates that clearly and kindly, without apology.

- Doesn't take on guilt when others are disappointed.

- Says no without spiraling.

- Asks for help before they collapse.

- Protects time for deep work, and for real rest.

- Doesn't equate worth with being constantly busy or available.

They are calm, respected, and trusted. People know where they stand. Their yes means something, because it's backed by intention, not pressure.

Boundaries aren't about distance. They're about clarity, and the clearer you are, the more powerful and peaceful you become.

How to Start (Even If You've Been Terrible at This)

So, what if you've never done this well? What if you've been the yes-person your whole career?

Start small.

Pick one boundary to set this week. Just one.

- Maybe it's no emails after 7pm.

- Maybe it's blocking two hours a day for deep work.

- Maybe it's saying no to one extra request that would push you over the edge.

When the guilt shows up, because it will, remind yourself: You're not being selfish. You're being smart.

Boundaries are a skill. And like any skill, you get better with practice. You start small. You build muscle. And soon enough, you'll look back and wonder how you ever worked without them.

This isn't about becoming inflexible. It's about becoming *intentional*. It's about deciding that your time, your energy, and your well-being matter, and acting accordingly.

You can be a great teammate and still say no. You can be a strong leader and still take care of yourself. You can be driven and still have boundaries.

And you should.

Without them? You're not helping anyone, especially not yourself.

Reflection Exercise: Your Boundary Blueprint

Take 10 minutes. Be honest. No one's grading this.

Where do you feel the most resentment at work?
(Resentment is a clue that a boundary is being ignored.)

What are you saying yes to that you know you shouldn't?
(What's draining your energy without returning value?)

What's one small boundary you could set this week?
(It doesn't have to be huge. Just meaningful.)

Who do you need to have a conversation with?
(And what's the simplest way to say it?)

What's the payoff for protecting your time and energy?
(Visualize the benefit. Make it real. That's your motivation.)

Write it down. Then try it. Start small and remember, this isn't about being perfect. It's about being *present*. For your work, your team, and yourself.

You don't need to earn rest. You just need to respect your limits. That starts now.

CHAPTER 14:
FEEDBACK, CRITICISM,
AND NOT TAKING
IT PERSONALLY

What if the thing you're most afraid to hear… is the thing you most need to hear?

Feedback is the breakfast of champions, or so they say. But let's be honest: most people treat it more like a plate of cold liver. They avoid it, dread it, and choke it down when they're forced to.

If you want to grow, as a teammate, a leader, or a person, feedback isn't optional. It's the mirror that helps you see what you normally can't. While it can sting (sometimes a lot), it's also one of the most powerful tools for transformation.

In this chapter, we're diving into how to take feedback without losing your shit, how to give it without causing a meltdown, and how to use it to build trust instead of breaking it.

Why Feedback Feels Like an Attack (Even When It's Not)

Let's start with the gut punch.

You get a message from your boss: "Can we talk?"

Your stomach drops. Your brain floods with panic. "What did I do?"

Sound familiar? That's your nervous system reacting to a perceived threat. It doesn't matter if you're a seasoned executive or an intern, the moment you hear the word "feedback," your body goes on high alert.

Why? Because feedback hits our identity.

Even when it's constructive, even when it's kind, it pokes at our sense of self. It challenges our story of who we think we are. If your self-worth is tightly wrapped around how people think about you at work, feedback can feel less like a helpful note and more like a personal attack.

Our brains are wired to interpret criticism as danger. In early human history, being rejected by the tribe could mean death. So when someone points out a flaw, even a small one, your brain reacts like you're about to be thrown out of the village.

That's why your heart races. Why your stomach clenches. Why your first instinct is often to defend, deflect, or shut down.

Signs you're taking feedback personally:

- You immediately start crafting excuses or justifications in your head.

- You get defensive, even if the feedback is accurate.

- You stew on the comment for days.

- You start doubting your abilities or questioning your value.

- You fixate on *who* said it instead of *what* they said.

Here's the thing: feedback isn't about your worth. It's about your impact.

You can be a good person, a hard worker, and still have blind spots. You can be doing your best and still be creating friction. You can be incredibly talented, and still have room to grow.

None of that makes you bad. It makes you human.

The sooner you can separate feedback from identity, the easier it becomes to receive, reflect, and evolve. Feedback isn't rejection, it's direction.

If you can learn to hear it, really hear it, without spiraling, you unlock one of the most powerful tools in your career.

But first, you have to stop seeing it as only a threat.

The Difference Between Criticism and Cruelty

Not all feedback is helpful, and not all criticism is constructive.

That's an important truth to acknowledge, especially if you've ever been burned by a boss who weaponized "feedback" to tear people down, or had a coworker who seemed more interested in pointing fingers than solving problems.

Before you decide that all feedback is cruel, let's make a critical distinction.

Criticism, when done well, is about *behavior* and *impact*. It's clear, specific, and intended to help someone improve. It names what isn't working and invites a conversation about how to fix it.

Cruelty, on the other hand, is about *control*, *judgment*, or *punishment*. It's vague. It's personal. It's often delivered in a moment of frustration or power flex. It leaves the other person feeling small instead of supported.

Criticism sounds like:

- "I think the presentation is a little long. Let's work on tightening up the key points."

- "You've missed a few deadlines, what's getting in the way?"

- "That email came across as abrupt. Let's talk about tone."

Cruelty sounds like:

- "I shouldn't have to explain this to you."

- "No one else seems to have a problem with this, just you."

- "If you can't figure this out, maybe this isn't the right job for you."

See the difference?

Good feedback focuses on the *work*, not the *worth* of the person doing it.

Some of the best feedback you'll ever get will sting a little. Not because it's cruel, but because it's honest. The truth has teeth. But cruelty? Cruelty is about power, not progress.

If someone's feedback leaves you feeling confused, diminished, or personally attacked, especially without a path forward, it's okay to question the delivery.

And if you're the one giving the feedback, check yourself:

- Are you naming the behavior, or attacking the person?

- Are you offering a path forward, or just venting?

- Are you calm and clear, or reactive and sharp?

The goal is to correct, not to crush. To help someone grow, not to shame them into silence.

Emotional Intelligence in the Moment

So you're sitting in that meeting, and someone drops feedback on you, expected or not. What happens next? That's where emotional intelligence becomes your superpower.

EQ is the difference between spiraling into defensiveness or shutting down, and actually hearing what's being said.

Step 1: Feel what you're feeling and name it.
Your jaw tightens. Your stomach drops. Maybe your brain starts racing. Don't ignore it. Notice it. Say to yourself: "I'm feeling defensive right now." That simple move calms your nervous system and puts your thinking brain back in charge.

Step 2: Breathe and pause.
Resist the urge to react right away. Even a two-second pause helps you re-center. Take a breath. Sip water. Say "Let me think about that for a second." You're not deflecting, you're controlling the response.

Step 3: Look for the signal, not just the noise.
Even in poorly delivered feedback, there's usually something useful. Find it. Don't waste energy judging the tone. Focus on the truth you might not have seen, or admitted, until now.

Step 4: Stay curious, not combative.
Ask a clarifying question:

- "Can you give me an example?"

- "How long have you noticed this?"

- "How does this affect the team?"

You're not trying to win. Ask because you're trying to learn.

Step 5: Thank them, then process privately.
Even if it's hard to hear, say, "Thanks for the feedback." Then go think. Don't make promises you're not ready to keep, but let them know you're open.

This level of composure? It's rare. It's powerful, and it will set you apart.

How to Actually Use Feedback

Here's where most people fail. They hear the feedback. They even write it down, and then? Nothing.

Growth doesn't come from hearing feedback. It comes from *using* it.

Here's how:

Reflect honestly. What part of the feedback stung, and why? Did it hit a nerve because it's true? Or because it challenged how you see yourself?

Look for the pattern. Was this a one-off comment? Or is it part of a theme? If three different managers over time have said you struggle with something, that's not a coincidence. That's a growth opportunity.

Identify the action. What's one thing you can start doing differently today? Be specific. "Be more collaborative" is vague. "Invite input in the first 15 minutes of meetings" is actionable.

Ask for help. If you're not sure how to improve, ask. "What would success look like here?" shows initiative and humility.

Check back in. Don't disappear after the feedback. After a few weeks, say: "I've been working on X, have you noticed a difference?" It shows maturity and signals that you're serious about growth.

That's how you transform feedback from a hit to your ego... into fuel for your evolution.

When Smart People Can't Take Feedback

Let's talk about the people you least expect to struggle with feedback: the high performers. The smart ones, the "stars."

Years ago, I had a product manager at a company I led, a brilliant guy. I mentioned a little about him earlier. He was sharp, creative, and had an almost obsessive focus on delivering results. On paper, he was a rockstar. In reality, he was a slow-moving train wreck.

There were signs. People came to me quietly, concerned. There were murmurs of missed deadlines, tension on the team, emotional outbursts. I brushed them off.

He's intense, I told myself. He's passionate, and he gets results.

But eventually, I couldn't ignore it. His relationships were crumbling. His team was miserable. Worst of all, when I tried to give him feedback, calm, thoughtful, honest feedback, he unraveled. He couldn't hear it.

It wasn't that the feedback was wrong. It was that his ego wouldn't let it in.

To him, feedback meant failure. It meant he wasn't the genius he believed himself to be. So he pushed it away, argued, deflected, and made endless excuses.

He lost everything, the trust, the team, the job.

It wasn't a skills issue. It was emotional intelligence, and the complete lack of it.

No matter how smart you are, if you can't take feedback, you'll hit a ceiling. You'll keep blowing up relationships, missing growth opportunities, and eventually... you'll be the common denominator in your own downfall.

Feedback doesn't kill careers, denial does.

Final Thoughts: Feedback Is a Gift (Even When It Sucks)

Here's the uncomfortable truth: You can't grow if you can't be corrected.

You can be the hardest worker in the room, the most technically brilliant, the most passionate, and still be limited by your inability to hear hard truths.

That's why this chapter matters.

Because feedback is one of the fastest paths to growth, but only if you let it be.

It's not always fair. It's not always delivered well. But when someone takes the time to tell you how you're showing up, you have two choices:

You can take it personally.

Or you can take it seriously.

Only one of those makes you better.

Reflection: Your Feedback Readiness Scorecard

Let's turn the mirror back on yourself. Use this moment to check in with how you currently handle feedback, and where you have room to grow.

Ask yourself:

- When was the last time I asked for feedback, without being forced to?

- What's my first emotional reaction when I hear something critical?

- Do I tend to get defensive, quiet, or dismissive?

- Have I ever written someone off after they gave me hard feedback?

- What would it look like if I treated feedback as a gift instead of a threat?

- What's one thing I've been avoiding hearing... because I already suspect it's true?

Growth starts when defensiveness ends. The more honest you can be here, the more powerful your next steps will be.

No one loves feedback at first. The people who learn to *use* it, instead of running from it, are the ones who grow the fastest, collaborate the best, and lead with the most impact.

That can be you.

CHAPTER 15: POWER DYNAMICS, POLITICS, AND PLAYING THE GAME (WITHOUT LOSING YOURSELF)

Working smart doesn't mean selling your soul. But it does mean learning how the game works.

The Unspoken Rules of Every Workplace

Every workplace has a rulebook. Most of it isn't written down.

Sure, there's an employee handbook. Org charts. Performance reviews. Job descriptions. Those aren't the rules that shape your day-to-day experience. The real force behind how work gets done are the unspoken rules: the ones you learn through experience, whispers, trial and error.

Who really makes decisions here? Who gets promoted, and who doesn't? Whose opinions are quietly ignored? What behaviors are tolerated, even if they're toxic?

These are the real questions that determine your experience at work, and your success within it.

The mistake many well-intentioned people make is assuming that doing great work is enough. It's just not. Great work is the baseline. Understanding how to navigate power, influence, and politics is what moves you forward (or keeps you stuck).

That's not cynical. That's reality.

If you don't learn how to read the room, you'll always be at the mercy of people who can. If you refuse to see how power flows through a company, you'll keep trying to swim upstream. If you don't understand the rules of the game, you'll keep wondering why it feels like you're losing, even when you're doing everything "right."

This chapter isn't about turning you into a manipulative operator. It's about giving you the tools to play the game without losing yourself in the process.

Whether you like it or not, you *are* a character in the game.

If you want to lead, influence, and thrive long-term, you'd better learn how to play it well.

Understanding Power: Titles vs. Influence

Most people assume power equals title. The higher you are on the org chart, the more power you have.

Now if you've spent any real time in business, you already know that's bullshit.

Power comes in many forms. Sometimes it's the assistant who manages the CEO's calendar and decides who gets face time. Sometimes it's the engineer who's been there ten years and holds the tribal knowledge of the entire product in their head. Sometimes it's the salesperson who hits 200% of quota and knows the CEO owes them more than a thank-you.

Influence doesn't always come with a title, and a title doesn't always mean influence.

Smart professionals figure out quickly: Who actually moves things here? Who has the ear of the decision-makers? Who can block a project with one sideways comment in a meeting?

Once you know that, you can start navigating reality, not just hierarchy.

If you want to grow your own influence, remember this: It's built through trust, clarity, consistency, and value. Show up well. Communicate clearly. Deliver reliably. And this is key, invest in relationships before you need them.

Reading the Room (And Why It Matters More Than You Think)

If emotional intelligence is the superpower of leadership, then reading the room is one of its highest expressions.

Reading the room means sensing what's really going on beneath the surface, not just what's being said. It means:

- Noticing who's being quiet in meetings.

- Picking up on tension between teams.

- Sensing when someone is threatened by your idea.

- Adjusting your message based on how it's landing.

This isn't about being fake. It's about being attuned.

There's a difference between being honest and being effective. Sometimes bluntness backfires. Sometimes the way you say something matters more than what you say. If you miss the social cues, the power signals or emotional climate, you're not going to land your message.

Learn to watch, and to listen. To pause before jumping in. To sense who needs space, who needs acknowledgment, who needs reassurance.

When you can read the room, you lead the room.

Managing Up Without Kissing Ass

You don't have to be a sycophant to have a good relationship with your boss, but you do have to manage the relationship.

Managing up means understanding what your manager needs to be successful, and helping them get there. It means understanding their communication style, their pressure points, their goals.

It doesn't mean being a doormat. It means being strategic.

Ask yourself:

- What does my boss care about most?

- What stresses them out?

- How can I make their life easier, without compromising my values?

When you learn to manage up effectively, your manager becomes your advocate, not your obstacle. You make their wins your wins. You create alignment. You earn trust.

When hard conversations come up, you've already built the foundation to have them.

Navigating Office Politics (Without Becoming a Politician)

"Office politics" gets a bad rap, but politics, in its most basic form, is just how people organize power and influence.

Avoiding office politics entirely doesn't make you noble. It makes you uninformed.

The key is to engage without compromising your integrity.

- Don't gossip, but do pay attention to what's being said.

- Don't manipulate, but do understand motivations.

- Don't play favorites, but do build alliances.

Stay out of petty drama, but don't isolate yourself. Stay above board, but not above awareness.

The people who say, "I don't do politics" often find themselves left out of the conversations that actually matter.

If you want a seat at the table, you have to learn what table you're actually sitting at.

Protecting Your Integrity in a Messy System

Here's the hardest truth: Good people can work in messy systems. Great leaders can operate under bad ones. Sometimes, the only way to make things better is to stay in the room without becoming part of the problem.

That's the real challenge of playing the game: holding on to your values when the environment doesn't reward them.

You're going to be tested. You'll see people cut corners and get promoted. You'll see toxic behavior ignored. You'll be tempted to say "screw it" and play dirty.

Real character shows up in moments of ambiguity. In the decisions no one sees. In how you treat people when you don't need anything from them.

You don't have to play dirty to win. But you do have to play smart.

And sometimes, playing smart means walking away from a system that's too broken to fix.

When You're the Underdog

Not everyone starts with the same access to power.

Some people are underestimated from day one. Maybe because

of how they look, or how they sound. Where they're from. What their title is. What degree they don't have. The baggage someone else is projecting onto them.

If that's you, this chapter matters even more.

Because you don't just have to be good. You have to be undeniable.

That means:

- Mastering your craft.

- Building relationships across levels.

- Staying grounded in your values.

- Advocating for yourself without apology.

And yes, it means learning the game so you can beat it, not be beaten by it.

You won't win every round. But over time, if you're consistent, strategic, and resilient, people will take notice.

Because excellence plus integrity? That's a combination they can't ignore forever.

What It Means to "Play the Game" (Without Losing Yourself)

Let's get real for a second.

A lot of people hear the phrase "play the game" and immediately recoil. It sounds manipulative, political, and inauthentic. Like you have to sell your soul just to succeed.

That's not what this chapter, or this book, is about.

Playing the game well doesn't mean becoming someone you're not. It means understanding the environment you're in and learning how to navigate it without getting eaten alive. It's self-awareness. It's emotional intelligence. It's strategic thinking, and yes, sometimes it's patience.

- It's knowing when to speak, and when to hold back.

- It's knowing how to disagree, without making it personal.

- It's knowing how to move people, even if they outrank you.

- It's knowing what battles to fight, and which ones to let go.

Playing the game well means understanding people.

If you've made it this far, you already know: people are messy. They're insecure. They're motivated by ego, fear, ambition, validation. They want to be seen, heard, respected, and when they're not, they act out in predictable ways.

So no, you don't have to kiss up. You don't have to sell out.

You *do* have to read the room. You *do* have to communicate in a way others can hear. You *do* have to understand what matters to your stakeholders, your boss, and your peers.

Most of all, you have to play long-term.

People who win in the short term by cutting corners, undercutting others, or weaponizing charm might seem successful, but those games don't last. Reputation catches up. Character shows. People remember how you made them feel.

So play the long game.

Be kind. Be clear. Be strategic. Be honest. Be someone who gets shit done *and* brings others with them.

That's what real influence looks like. That's how you build something that lasts. That's how you win, without losing yourself.

Reflection: How Are You

Playing the Game?

Take a few minutes and ask yourself:

- Do I understand the unspoken rules of my workplace?

- Am I paying attention to how power flows, or pretending it doesn't matter?

- Where am I resisting the game, and why?

- Where am I playing it poorly, and what is that costing me?

- What's one move I can make this week to lead with more clarity, influence, or strategy?

You don't have to become a politician. But if you want to lead, if you want to build something meaningful, you'd better understand how the game works.

You'd better learn how to play it like someone who still sleeps well at night.

You've Looked in the Mirror. Now Let's Build Something Better.

Now take a moment, seriously. Most people never do this work. They never stop to reflect. Never question their defaults. Never ask how they might be making it harder for themselves, or everyone around them. That is what you are doing now.

You looked in the mirror and stayed. You faced the ego, the fear, the dysfunction. You stopped blaming, started owning, and maybe even saw yourself, clearly, for the first time in a long time.

Now comes the real work. Awareness without action is just a therapy session. What you've uncovered in Part 1 and Part 2? That's your foundation. Now it's time to bring it home.

Part 3: Bring It All Together

This is the part where you stop sucking and start leading.

By now, you've looked inward. You've seen how fear, ego, and misalignment show up in you, and in everyone around you. You've learned how to navigate workplace chaos without being swallowed by it. You've sharpened your self-awareness, figured out how to survive dysfunction, and (hopefully) stopped blaming your boss for everything.

This part of the book is where we take everything you've learned and put it into practice. Not just to keep your head above water, but to swim like a pro, maybe even help others do the same. This is where we talk about structure, trust, culture, and the kind of leadership that doesn't just work, it lasts.

You don't have to be a manager to lead. You don't need a title to set the tone. You just need the willingness to go first. Let's bring it home.

CHAPTER 16: LEAD YOURSELF FIRST

Before you lead anyone else, get your own house in order.

Leadership isn't a title. It's how you show up when things go sideways.

It's easy to talk about leadership when everything's going smoothly, when your team is aligned, your project is on track, and your coffee was made right. Real leadership shows up when you're tired, frustrated, blindsided, or under pressure. In those moments, you can't fake it. You lead from what's inside you.

That's why this chapter comes first in Part 3. If you want to lead others well, you have to start with yourself. Your habits. Your emotions. Your tone. Your triggers. Your default reactions when things don't go to plan.

You can have the best strategy in the world, but if you're reactive, inconsistent, or emotionally erratic, your team won't trust you. They won't feel safe. They won't follow you.

This chapter is about building that steady core, so that when things do go sideways (and they will), you don't spiral. You lead.

Emotional Regulation Is Leadership

There have been countless moments in my career as a technology executive when things have gone completely sideways, the kind of situations that would make anyone's pulse spike. The entire site is offline. A high-stakes cloud migration has taken an unexpected turn, and there's no easy way back. We are 100% not ready, and the President and CEO of the company are in New York in an RV ready to do people's tax returns in Times Square. In those moments, I've learned one critical truth: your team is watching you.

They're not just waiting for instructions. They're looking for a signal. Are we panicking? Are we in trouble? Is this fixable?

If you lose it, they lose it.

So I've learned to pause. To take 30 seconds, just 30 seconds, to breathe, calm my body, and think. That moment of composure never hurts you. It only helps. In these situations, doing nothing doesn't solve anything, and rushing headfirst without clarity can make it worse.

Instead, I think: What's the first thing that needs to happen? Do I have the right people involved? What are our options? Then I act, carefully, calmly, and decisively, to get the damn thing back online and back on track.

That's emotional regulation. That's leadership.

Let's get this out of the way: You're not ChatGPT. You're human. You're allowed to have feelings: anger, frustration, disappointment, and anxiety.

But your job as a leader is to *process* those feelings, not *project* them.

If you're snapping at your team because your exec meeting went poorly, that's not leadership. That's displacement. If your tone changes every time you're stressed, your people learn to walk on eggshells. They don't know who they're getting day to day, and that unpredictability kills trust.

Leaders who can stay calm under pressure aren't suppressing emotions, they've learned to *regulate* them. To recognize when their stress is creeping in. To take a breath before responding.

To say, "Let me get back to you on that," when they feel flooded instead of exploding or ghosting.

If you want your team to stay grounded, it starts with you.

Set the Emotional Temperature

You've probably heard that leaders set the tone. It's deeper than that. You set the *emotional temperature* of the room. Your presence influences everyone else's state.

If you walk into a meeting frantic and unfocused, your team absorbs that. If you lead with clarity and calm, even when things are messy, people breathe easier.

Think of yourself as the thermostat, not the thermometer. Don't just react to the heat, *set* the temperature. This doesn't mean pretending everything is fine when it's not. It means showing up with intentional energy.

If you want a thoughtful team, be thoughtful. If you want a team that owns their mistakes, model accountability. If you want a team that doesn't spiral in chaos, show them how to anchor. If you feel it is right to turn up the heat, then do it intentionally, not emotionally.

Your behavior gives everyone else permission to rise, or to retreat.

Stop Defaulting to Chaos

If your default mode is sprinting from one fire to the next, overpromising and under-recovering, constantly "catching up," you're not leading, you're leaking.

Burnout is not a badge of honor. Reactivity is not a strategy. Being overwhelmed doesn't make you important. It makes you ineffective.

Great leaders create margin for themselves and others. They plan, and reflect. They slow down enough to see clearly. They don't let urgency turn every task into a crisis. They understand the cost of running on fumes, and they refuse to make it the norm.

If you're always in chaos, your team will be too.

Want to lead well? Step off the hamster wheel. Create space to think. Build systems that prevent chaos instead of worshiping it.

Check Your Settings

You can't control everything, but you can check your settings.

Before a meeting, ask yourself:

- What do I want this person to feel when they leave?

- What energy am I bringing in?

- Am I projecting stress I haven't dealt with yet?

End-of-day check:

- What did I bring to the room today?

- Where did I lead well, and where did I react?

- What do I need to reset before tomorrow?

These micro-reflections take five minutes, but they build awareness, and awareness builds leadership.

The more you understand how *you* are showing up, the more intentionally you can lead.

The Leader You Are When No One's Watching

Here's the final gut check: Who are you when it's just you?

When no one's asking for updates. When no one's watching how you treat that "less important" person. When no one's there to see whether you step up, or check out.

Here's a great test: how do you work when your boss isn't around? Not just when they're in back-to-back meetings, but when they're out for the day. When you're working on something that doesn't have a deadline. When no one's hovering over your shoulder. Do you coast? Do you procrastinate, or do you hold yourself to the same standard you expect from others?

Real leadership, the kind that earns trust and inspires others, starts in the moments no one is watching. It's when you clean up a mess someone else left. It's when you choose to do the deeper, more thoughtful version of the work instead of the checkbox version. It's when you meet your own expectations even when no one is checking.

If you want to be a leader people trust, a leader people choose to follow, you have to lead yourself first.

Reflection: Are You Leading Yourself?

- When was the last time I checked in with my emotional state before a conversation?

- How do I respond when I'm under pressure?

- What tone do I bring into the room most often?

- Do people feel safer, calmer, or more focused after interacting with me?

- What's one self-leadership habit I can commit to this week?

You don't need to be perfect. But you do need to be aware. Because how you show up sets the stage for everything that follows.

If you can lead yourself well, consistently, you've already won half the battle.

CHAPTER 17: STRUCTURE KILLS CHAOS (AND BUILDS TRUST)

Why Chaos Isn't Creative (It's Just Confusing)

There's a romanticized idea in some circles that chaos is the birthplace of genius. That if you just remove the rules, keep things loose, and let people "figure it out," magic will happen.

Sometimes maybe it does, but most of the time? People spiral, deadlines slip, priorities shift, and meetings turn into guessing games. The people you *want* to keep? They will burn out or check out.

Chaos doesn't create, it corrodes.

When people don't know what's expected of them, they default to self-protection. They work on what they feel most confident in. They second-guess decisions. They slow down, or worse, speed up in the wrong direction.

The idea that structure stifles creativity is a myth. In reality, structure gives creativity a runway. It gives people room to focus, collaborate, and execute with confidence. They're no longer wasting energy figuring out what matters, or who owns what.

What Structure Actually Looks Like

Let's get something clear: structure is not micromanagement. It's not a 47-step process for sending an email. It's not checking on your team every 10 minutes to ask for updates.

Structure is alignment.

It's the shared understanding of:

- What matters most right now.

- Who owns what.

- What "done" looks like.

- How we stay connected.

Structure shows up in simple things:

- A recurring Monday priorities meeting with clear outcomes.

- A project tracker that everyone updates weekly.

- Defined roles so no one's stepping on each other's toes.

- A 15-minute end-of-week retro to discuss what worked and what didn't.

You don't need to build a fortress. You need to build a framework, something that gives people a strong foundation and room to move.

Think structure slows people down? Ask yourself how much time your team loses every week to miscommunication, rework, or vague direction.

The Emotional Power of Clarity

Structure isn't just an operational tool. It's an emotional one.

When people are clear on what's expected, when it's due, and how to succeed, they breathe easier. They focus. They stop wondering if they're dropping the ball. They stop fearing that they'll be blindsided in a meeting.

Clarity makes people feel safe, not because they're being coddled, but because they're being respected. They know where they stand. They know what matters. They can measure themselves against something real, not shifting goalposts and gut feelings.

Ambiguity, on the other hand, is a stressor. It leads to anxiety, silence, and passive-aggression. People don't raise their hands because they're afraid they're supposed to already know the answer. They start hedging instead of collaborating. They look busy instead of being productive, because in a world without clarity, performance becomes theater.

When leaders provide structure, they reduce cognitive load. That frees people up to *do the work* instead of constantly *interpreting the work*.

If you think your team should "just know", stop. They don't. Not because they're not smart, but because they don't live in your head. You owe them clarity, and they owe it to each other.

Want people to trust you? Give them clarity.

How to Set Clear Expectations (Without Being a Jerk)

Some leaders avoid structure because they're afraid of sounding bossy. Others go too far and end up sounding like a taskmaster.

Here's the middle ground: clear expectations, delivered collaboratively.

Use this simple framework when assigning anything:

- **What** exactly needs to be done?

- **When** is it due, or when should we check in?

- **Why** does this matter? What's the context?

- **Who** should they go to if they get stuck?

For example:

"I'd love for you to lead the deck for the Q2 marketing strategy review. We need a draft by next Wednesday so we can all give initial feedback on Thursday. I want this to help us drive sharper focus across the organization, especially around marketing spend. If you get blocked, talk to Casey or shoot me a note."

That's structure. That's leadership. It doesn't sound robotic or bossy. It just sounds clear.

When Structure Is Missing: The Signs

Want to know if your team is lacking structure? Don't look at your project plan. Look at the people.

Here are the red flags:

- **People are firefighting all the time.** Everything is urgent. Nothing is prioritized.

- **You hear the phrase "I thought you were doing that."** Ownership is vague.

- **Projects drag or stall out.** Momentum disappears.

- **People duplicate effort.** Teams are solving the same problems in silos.

- **Tension is rising.** People are anxious, short-tempered, or going quiet.

These are emotional signals of operational disorganization.

And you know what else shows up? Exhaustion. The quiet kind. The kind that builds when people don't know what success looks like, when they aren't sure whether they're winning or losing, when the bar keeps moving. That slow, frustrating erosion of confidence, not just in the system, but in themselves.

You'll see great people start second-guessing every decision. You'll see high performers drift, disconnect, or quit without warning. Not because they weren't committed, but because the environment was too disorienting to navigate any longer.

This isn't a people problem. It's a structural problem. You don't fix it with a pep talk or another all-hands meeting. You fix it by putting the right anchors in place.

You don't fix them with a speech. You fix them with structure.

Build Systems That People Can Actually Use

The best systems are the ones people actually use, consistently.

They're not built to impress. They're built to function. If you have a dozen dashboards that no one opens, a 300-slide playbook no one reads, or a weekly meeting that feels like a hostage situation, that's not structure. That's just noise.

Good systems support clarity, momentum, and trust. They get out of the way and help people stay connected without overwhelming them.

You don't need to adopt some elaborate project management suite or force everyone to follow a rigid methodology. You just need tools that support clear communication, shared ownership, and ongoing visibility.

Some ideas:

- **Weekly priorities check-ins.** Everyone lists 3–5 things they're focused on.

- **Daily 60-second standups.** Everyone shares what they're working on and what's blocking them.

- **Shared documents with clear roles and deadlines.** Use comments. Keep it live.

- **Project kickoff templates.** Align on what success looks like before anyone starts working.

- **End-of-week wrap-ups.** One-line summaries of what moved, what didn't, and why.

Keep it lightweight. Keep it visible, and keep it real.

The goal isn't control. It's coordination. It's creating a rhythm your team can rely on, even in the face of shifting priorities and fast-moving decisions.

If your systems aren't helping, fix them. If they're slowing you down, simplify them. And if no one's using them? Start over, with your people, not just your software.

Because great systems don't just improve productivity. They reduce stress, build alignment, and let people actually do their best work.

When to Flex the Structure (Without Breaking It)

Structure is a guide, not a cage.

Sometimes you'll need to adapt. A project scope changes. A teammate gets pulled into something urgent. A timeline moves. That's life.

Flexibility doesn't mean chaos. It means conscious adjustments, communicated clearly, and understood as *exceptions*, not defaults.

When you flex, be explicit:

- "We're skipping the retro this week so the team can focus on the launch. We'll double back next week."

- "Let's move that deadline to Friday so we can incorporate the new data."

Don't let exceptions become the new normal. Flex with intention, not because the structure was never real to begin with.

It's also important to understand the difference between being adaptable and being disorganized. If your team is constantly flexing, it may be a sign that your structure was never solid to begin with. Flexibility should support high performance, not serve as a smokescreen for lack of planning.

Set boundaries around what is truly negotiable and what is non-negotiable. When you flex, revisit the structure to determine if it needs to evolve, not disappear.

Done well, structure evolves with your team. It gets smarter, not sloppier. More human, not more chaotic.

Reflection: Where Is Chaos Costing You?

- Where is ambiguity showing up in my team or process?

- What systems are missing, or overly complex?

- Where am I tolerating vagueness in expectations?

- What's one small structure I can implement this week to bring more clarity?

Structure isn't about control. It's about care.

When you give people clarity, you give them confidence. You give them space to grow. You build the kind of trust that lasts, even when everything else changes.

CHAPTER 18: SAY THE THING

Hard conversations aren't the problem. Avoiding them is.

Let's get this out of the way: saying the thing doesn't mean being an asshole.

It means being clear and direct. Speaking like an adult, especially when it's uncomfortable.

Let's be honest. We all know someone who's great at this. Probably someone's grandparent. You ask if they like your new haircut and they respond immediately, "It's not your best." They're not trying to be rude, they just don't see the point in pretending. They've seen enough, lived enough, and dealt with enough to know that tiptoeing around the truth rarely helps anyone. That's what happens when you stop caring about being liked and start caring about being useful.

We could all use a little of that grandma energy.

The truth is, most dysfunction at work isn't caused by bad intentions. It's caused by what people won't say. Feedback never gets delivered. Boundaries never get set. Expectations were never clear in the first place.

We avoid saying the thing because we don't want to be uncomfortable. But that discomfort doesn't disappear. It festers. The longer we wait, the messier it gets.

Let's fix that.

The Real Cost of Not Saying It

Avoiding hard conversations might feel safer in the moment, but it always costs more in the long run.

It costs clarity, performance, and trust. It usually leads to a much harder conversation later, when someone's already frustrated, burned out, or on their way out the door.

Here's what silence actually communicates:

- "I don't care enough to address this."

- "I don't trust you with the truth."

- "This problem isn't worth solving."

None of those are things you mean. But if you're not saying the thing, that's what's being heard.

Avoidance doesn't just create confusion. It creates resentment. Ironically, the longer you wait to say something, the harder it becomes to say it well.

One of the biggest lessons I've learned in leadership, and painfully, more than once, is that clarity delayed becomes damage multiplied. This is still a key skill set I work on constantly.

Why Adults Say the Thing

Saying the thing doesn't mean being aggressive. It means being honest and speaking with respect.

People deserve to know where they stand. They deserve to know when something's not working, whether it's performance, collaboration, attitude, or alignment. They deserve a chance to improve or respond before decisions get made without them.

The most respectful thing you can do as a leader, or even just as a teammate, is to stop pretending everything's fine when it's not.

Say it clearly, early, and directly. Not weeks later, laced with resentment and built-up frustration.

I've had moments where I knew something was off. A team lead was slipping. Deadlines were getting missed. Energy was off. convinced myself I'd "let it play out" or "give it more time." By the time I finally said something, the dynamic had already gone south, and it felt like an ambush.

I wasn't being kind by waiting. I was procrastinating and being avoidant.

The most adult conversations are the ones that happen *before* a situation becomes a crisis.

Common Communication Cop-Outs (and What to Do Instead)

You've probably used one of these. We all have.

The Vague Feedback

"You just need to be more proactive."

What does that even mean? To the person hearing it, it sounds like a judgment with no action.

Try this instead:

"I noticed you waited to be pulled into that project rather than stepping up early. In your role, I'd love to see you raise your hand sooner and take initiative when you see something that needs support."

The Compliment Sandwich

"You're great. Just one thing. But really, you're doing amazing."

It confuses people. They don't know what the actual message is, or how seriously to take it.

Be kind and direct. Say the real thing with care, not fluff.

The Late Night Email Novel

Ten paragraphs of emotionally charged rambling, sent at 10:47 p.m.

Don't hide behind the keyboard. If something matters, it probably deserves a conversation. Real-time, human-to-human.

When You Don't Know What to Say

It's okay to start with: "This is a little awkward, but I think it's important." That honesty breaks the ice, and invites connection, not conflict.

How to Say It Without Burning the Place Down

Here's your guide:

- **Tone over script.** If you come in hot, even the best message lands like an attack. Bring steady energy. If you're nervous or unsure, lead with that honesty: "I want to talk through something, I'm still figuring out how to say it well, but I don't want to avoid it." That alone disarms people.

- **Start with curiosity.** "Can we talk about what happened in the meeting yesterday? I noticed some tension and I want to understand it better." Asking instead of assuming keeps people from getting defensive.

- **Stick to behavior, not character.** Say what happened and how it impacted the work. Avoid labels or assumptions. "You interrupted three times in that conversation, which made it hard for others to contribute" is much better than "You dominate meetings."

- **Make space.** Let the other person speak, and listen. Then adjust. Don't treat your message like a verdict.

Also, practice makes perfect. If saying hard things doesn't come naturally to you, write it out first. Say it out loud to yourself. Ask a trusted peer to sanity-check your language. This isn't about perfection. It's about clarity with care.

Timing matters. Don't bring up performance issues at 4:58 p.m. on a Friday. Don't dump feedback into a message thread on a Sunday night. Set yourself, and them, up for success. Give the conversation a time and space where people can actually process it.

Finally, remember this: you're not trying to "win" the conversation. You're trying to move things forward. A hard conversation that creates clarity and momentum is a win for everyone.

Hard conversations that are handled well *build* trust, because they show you care enough to tell the truth and respect the relationship enough to do it with skill.

Say It Sooner

There's a golden window for hard conversations, and most of us miss it. Not because we don't care, but because we hesitate. We second-guess. We hope it'll work itself out. We want to give someone the benefit of the doubt. We want to avoid "making it a big thing."

But here's the truth: if it's on your mind, it's already a thing.

When you say the thing early, it's often a small, honest course correction. When you wait too long, it becomes a confrontation, and people rarely respond well to being surprised by criticism they didn't see coming.

Early is kind, useful, and professional.

Think of it like steering a ship. One degree off course isn't a big deal, unless you wait a few hundred miles. Then you're in a different ocean.

Small feedback, given early, avoids the giant course correction later. It also keeps emotions from boiling over and makes space for growth without shame.

When you model that for others, it starts to spread. Your team learns that feedback isn't a punishment. It's a tool. It's normal, and expected. Eventually, it becomes part of the culture, not a crisis.

When You've Waited Too Long

Sometimes you miss the window. You didn't say anything, and now it's blown up. The pattern is repeating. The trust is fraying. The silence is loud.

So what do you do? You own it.

You don't pretend the issue just started. You don't act like your frustration came out of nowhere. You name the delay.

"I should've brought this up earlier. That's on me. I wanted to give it space, but I realize now that I've waited too long to address it clearly."

That one sentence resets the tone. It shows maturity. It shows accountability. It makes space for the other person to stay open instead of getting defensive.

Because here's what happens when we don't own the delay, the conversation feels like a blindside. The other person feels ambushed, and you've now made the issue harder than it had to be.

You can recover, but only if you stop pretending everything's fine. Say it. Say that you waited. Say why. Then get back to the behavior, the impact, and the solution.

I once had a senior executive on my team who was showing signs of burnout, disorganization, broken commitments, and defensiveness. I didn't want to micromanage. I didn't want to overreact. I knew this person had value, and I told myself they'd pull it together.

By the time I finally sat down to address the pattern, I realized I had missed dozens of signs, and they'd made promises to their team they couldn't deliver on. Morale had taken a hit. I had to clean up something I could have prevented. That's on me.

The truth? Most hard conversations are easier than the consequences of avoiding them.

What Happens When You Start Saying the Thing

Here's the part most people don't expect: when you start saying the thing, clearly, calmly, respectfully, everything gets easier.

You don't carry resentment around like a weight. You don't spend energy spinning scenarios in your head. The tension doesn't simmer and poison your working relationships.

Instead, you build trust. Real trust, the kind that says, "We can be honest with each other." You give people a chance to meet your expectations, instead of guessing at them. You stop bottling up discomfort and start modeling maturity.

Your team learns they don't have to fear feedback. They learn it's possible to be direct and human at the same time. They start bringing things to you sooner. They start saying the thing, too.

You don't need everyone to like what you say, but if they trust *why* and *how* you say it, they'll listen. Then over time, they'll follow.

Because clarity, delivered with care, is leadership.

The more you practice it, the more it becomes part of who you are, not just what you do when backed into a corner.

Reflection: What Aren't You Saying?

- What conversation have I been avoiding, and why?

- What's the impact of my silence on the other person? On the work?

- What's one sentence I can say to open the conversation?

- How would I want someone to approach *me* if the roles were reversed?

You don't need the perfect words. You just need to care enough to be clear.

Say the thing. Say it like an adult, and say it in time.

CHAPTER 19:
BUILDING A CULTURE
THAT DOESN'T SUCK

Culture isn't what you say. It's what you do (and tolerate).

What Culture Actually Is (And Isn't)

Let's start with a myth: culture is not your mission statement.

It's not the slick brand video or the words painted on the conference room wall. It's not the team happy hour or the messaging channel where people share dog memes. Those things might reflect the culture, or they might just be window dressing.

Culture is what happens when no one's watching.

It's how people treat each other in meetings. It's how feedback is given (or avoided). It's whether people speak up when something's broken. It's whether people feel safe being honest, or whether they learn to stay quiet.

Culture isn't created in onboarding. It's revealed in pressure.

When a deadline is missed, how do people respond? When there's conflict, do people go direct or go silent? When someone makes a mistake, is it treated like a learning opportunity, or a character flaw?

That's the culture.

It's not about the perks. It's not about the software stack. It's not about whether you're remote, hybrid, or back in the office three days a week.

Culture is the emotional and behavioral tone of your team. It's what people come to expect, from each other, from leadership, and from the system as a whole.

Still wondering what that means in practical terms? Think of culture as the quality of three core functions:

- **Communication**, How we speak, share, respond, and listen.

- **Collaboration**, How we work together, solve conflict, share ownership, and make decisions.

- **Community**, How people feel they belong, contribute, and are seen within the group.

If your communication is unclear, your collaboration is messy, and your community is built on cliques, you're going to have a dysfunctional culture, even if your results look okay on paper.

We talked earlier in this book about the company as a living organism. Culture is the oxygen. It allows the system to breathe, grow, and thrive. When your culture is toxic, it's like cutting off airflow. The organism gets sick. It struggles, breaks down, or starts amputating limbs to survive.

Every team has a culture, whether you're paying attention to it or not.

How Culture Forms

We said "every team has a culture." The only question is whether it was built on purpose, or by accident.

Culture forms in the spaces between the big moments. It's not created by a single offsite or declared by leadership at the quarterly all-hands. Culture is shaped every day, by small actions repeated over time. Often, the things that shape it most aren't the things written down, they're the things people pick up on.

Culture forms through:

- **Repetition:** What happens over and over becomes the norm.

- **Observation:** People learn what matters by watching what gets praised, ignored, or punished.

- **Stories:** The tales people tell about how things really work here, not what's written in the handbook.

You can say your culture values collaboration, but if promotions always go to the loudest lone wolf, that's your real culture.

You can say your culture values transparency, but if people are punished for telling the truth or asking hard questions, your culture says otherwise.

And you can say your culture values trust, but if no one ever admits when they're stuck or unsure, the actual culture is fear.

Culture is like gravity: it's always shaping behavior, whether you're thinking about it or not. If you're not actively defining and reinforcing it, then the default behaviors, the passive, easy, sometimes toxic ones, will take over.

Inaction is action. Every time you ignore a bad habit, a poor communicator, or a behavior that goes against the values you claim to uphold, you're reinforcing a standard. Once *that* standard takes hold, it spreads.

That's how culture forms, not by proclamation, but by pattern.

The Culture Equation: What You Allow = What You Are

Culture is created not by what you say you value, but by what you're willing to tolerate.

You can build an elaborate onboarding program. You can publish core values in every conference room. But if you allow someone to steamroll meetings, undercut colleagues, or ignore deadlines without consequences, that behavior becomes the culture.

What gets repeated becomes normal. What gets tolerated becomes endorsed. What gets ignored becomes contagious.

The worst behaviors on a team rarely start as huge violations. They start small, a passive-aggressive email, a missed deadline, a disrespectful joke. And when nothing happens? That silence becomes permission.

Your culture is not defined by your top performers. It's defined by what your worst behavior says about your standards.

So what are you letting slide? Do people show up late to meetings and no one says a word? Are deadlines treated like soft suggestions instead of commitments? Are people allowed to speak in toxic or dismissive ways without accountability, because they "get results"? Does leadership sexually harass their workers? Those behaviors are your culture.

And the examples don't stop there:

- Is management okay with beers on Fridays at 5 p.m., until it becomes 4 p.m., then 3 p.m.?

- Are lunch breaks quietly stretching from 30 minutes to 90 minutes without a word?

- Is there someone who regularly comes back from lunch smelling like a brewery and nobody says anything?

Those aren't quirks. Those are signals. And they're telling your entire team what's really okay around here.

You can only create a culture of excellence by being excellent. That doesn't mean perfect. It means intentional. You either raise the standard through your example and enforcement, or you slowly bring it down through your silence.

One toxic person doesn't just annoy people, they rewire the whole system. Good people withdraw. High performers stop contributing. New hires learn quickly to play it safe instead of stepping up.

If you're not addressing harmful behavior, you're training everyone to lower their bar.

And this isn't just about leadership. Everyone contributes. When you stay silent in the face of dysfunction, even if you're not the manager, you're feeding the problem. Your silence makes noise.

So if you want a better culture, ask yourself: what are you tolerating?

Because that's what you're teaching.

Culture Starts With You (Even If You're Not "The Boss")

You don't need a fancy title or a corner office to influence culture. In fact, some of the most powerful culture-shapers in any organization are the people without formal authority, the team members who lead through example, not position.

Culture is shaped every time you:

- Speak up respectfully in a meeting instead of staying silent.

- Ask for feedback and take it seriously.

- Thank someone for their work, even when you didn't have to.

- Hold yourself accountable when you mess up.

These are leadership moves, and they don't require permission.

If you're on a team, your tone, effort, and values show up every day. They tell others what kind of space this is. Whether this is a place where people speak honestly, where it's safe to admit mistakes. Whether it's okay to ask questions or challenge decisions.

You might think you're just "one person," but culture spreads through people like you. You can be the reason someone stays. The reason someone speaks up. The reason someone trusts the team again.

So stop waiting for culture to be handed down. Stop saying, "That's just how it is around here."

Start showing people what it could be, by how you show up.

Culture is contagious, and you get to choose what you're spreading.

Repairing a Culture That's Gone Sideways

Sometimes the culture isn't what you hoped it would be. Maybe you inherited a mess. Things drifted while you were heads-down in survival mode. Maybe you just weren't paying attention, and now the tone of your team feels off.

Here's the good news: culture can be rebuilt, but it takes intention, consistency, and a whole lot of honesty.

Start by listening. If your team has grown quiet, frustrated, or disengaged, they already know what's broken. Don't start with solutions. Start with questions:

- "What's working and what's not?"

- "What do you wish we did more of, or less of?"

- "What would make this a place you're proud to be part of?"

Then, and this is the hard part, don't defend. Don't justify. Don't minimize, listen.

From there, pick your priorities. You can't fix everything overnight, but you can start somewhere. Maybe it's revamping feedback loops, or clarifying expectations. Perhaps it's finally addressing the behavior everyone's been tiptoeing around.

The next step is setting new norms, and sticking to them. It doesn't matter if you write a brilliant cultural manifesto if you don't enforce the basics:

- We start meetings on time.

- We give direct feedback.

- We treat people with respect, even when we disagree.

When people see the new standard being upheld consistently, especially when it's inconvenient, trust starts to rebuild. But if you slip back into silence or slide into old patterns, people will stop believing the change is real.

Repairing culture is like healing trust: it's slow, intentional work, but it's worth it.

The alternative, staying in a broken culture, costs you your best people, your best work, and your own peace.

Protecting a Culture That's Actually Working

When your culture is finally in a good place, it can be tempting to coast. That's when erosion starts. Great culture isn't a one-time win, it's an ongoing practice.

You protect it by reinforcing what's working:

- Celebrate healthy collaboration.

- Call out quiet leadership and small wins.

- Thank the people who model the values, especially when no

one's watching.

You also protect culture by watching for decay:

- Apathy creeping in.

- Toxic behavior going unchecked.

- New hires adopt bad habits because "that's just how we do it."

It only takes a few weeks of silence to undo months of progress.

If you've worked hard to build a culture that feels human, honest, and functional, guard it. Make the case for it. Speak up when something threatens it. Don't be afraid to be the person who says, "That's not how we do things here."

A great culture isn't self-sustaining. It's stewarded.

The teams that protect their culture, fiercely and proudly, are the ones people never want to leave.

Reflection: What Kind of Culture Are You Building?

Take 10 minutes to sit with these questions. Journal them, and discuss them with your team. Don't rush them, culture only changes when we do.

- What behaviors do I consistently reward, tolerate, or ignore?

- Where have I allowed standards to drift, and why?

- What's one cultural pattern on my team I'm proud of? How do I protect and amplify it?

- What's one cultural issue we're tolerating that needs to be addressed?

- How do people feel after working with me?

- What's one thing I can say or do this week to reinforce the culture we *want*, not just the one we have?

Remember, culture isn't a poster on the wall. It's what happens every day.

So make it count.

CHAPTER 20:
BUILDING A TEAM
THAT DOESN'T SUCK

The team you build is a reflection of the leadership you bring.

A quick note before we dive in: This chapter is especially useful for hiring managers, team builders, department leads, or anyone making decisions about who gets brought into the organization. If that's not your role (yet), don't skip it. Understanding what strong hiring, onboarding, and accountability *should* look like helps you spot good leadership, and eventually model it yourself.

Hire for Alignment, Not Just Skillset

Let's be honest: hiring is hard, and hiring fast is dangerous.

When you're under pressure to fill a seat, it's tempting to focus on experience, credentials, and whether the person seems "qualified." But here's the thing: the worst hiring mistakes aren't about skills. They're about alignment.

Does this person share the values of your team? Do they work well under the kind of pressure your company is facing? Do they know how to take feedback, course-correct, and contribute without ego?

Because if they don't, it doesn't matter how sharp their resume is. They'll drag your team backwards.

Hire for how they work, not just what they know.

That means listening for mindset. Watch how they talk about former teammates or previous managers. Are they reflective or blamey? Do they talk like a collaborator or a solo hero? Are they coachable?

You want culture-adds, people who bring something new while aligning with what matters. "Culture fit" has been misused for too long to mean "people just like us."

Some red flags you should never ignore:

- They talk about every past job like they were the victim.

- They can't name a mistake they've made.

- They dismiss soft skills as irrelevant.

- They give vague answers about how they solve problems or receive feedback.

One of the best indicators of how someone will work with *you* is how they've worked with people before. People don't suddenly become accountable, humble, or empathetic because they switched companies.

Hiring is your chance to shape the culture, protect it like it matters. Because it does.

When you're interviewing, don't just ask about projects and results. Ask questions that reveal how they respond to challenge, conflict, and criticism:

- What makes you angry at work?

- When was the last time you were rightly criticized by a manager? How did you handle it?

- Have you ever had to give difficult feedback to someone? How did it go, and how did you feel about it?

- Do you typically get along with your coworkers? Why or why not?

You're not just looking for polished answers. You're looking for emotional intelligence. For reflection. For how they view themselves in the context of a team.

These kinds of questions cut through the performance and get to the real human you're about to put inside the organism that is your company. If they're already defensive, dismissive, or surface-level in an interview, don't assume they'll get better once they're on payroll.

Interviewing isn't just about selling someone on your company. It's about protecting your team from bringing in someone who doesn't match what you're building.

Set People Up for Success (Not Mystery)

Too many managers treat onboarding like a talent test. They drop someone into the deep end and wait to see if they can swim. Spoiler: that's not leadership. That's laziness.

Your new hires want to succeed. Most of them are showing up on day one with optimism and energy. Your job is to give them a runway, not a riddle.

That means being painfully clear about:

- What their actual responsibilities are.

- What success looks like in the first 30, 60, and 90 days.

- How decisions get made.

- Who they can go to for help.

- How feedback will be delivered (and when).

This might sound like a lot, but clarity is kindness. You're not micromanaging. You're showing them the map.

Want to know what derails promising new employees? It's not a lack of talent. It's uncertainty or silence. It's unclear priorities and expectations that only exist in your head.

When people don't know what good looks like, they start second-guessing everything. They hesitate. They shrink. Or worse, they guess wrong, and now you're frustrated and they're confused.

The first few weeks of someone's job set the tone for everything that follows. That includes how safe they feel to ask questions, how quickly they bond with the team, and whether they trust your leadership enough to bring their full selves to work.

So yes, take the time to document the basics. Have the 1-on-1s. Give the early feedback. Share the context.

Because success isn't just what people *do*. It's what they *understand*.

Accountability on a Healthy Team

Accountability gets a bad rap. As we discussed earlier, too many people hear the word and think it means punishment. But true accountability isn't about control, it's about clarity, trust, and follow-through.

On a healthy team, accountability means:

- Everyone knows what their role is.

- Everyone understands how their work connects to the team's goals.

- Everyone follows through, or raises their hand early if they can't.

- And everyone is willing to be held to the same standard, including the leaders.

When accountability is present, things move. Conversations are clearer. Projects get done faster. People trust each other more. Trust isn't just about believing someone won't screw up. It's about knowing that when they *do*, they'll own it and fix it.

If you're a leader, your job is to make accountability a habit, not a surprise. That means building systems that make ownership visible. Weekly check-ins. Clear deliverables. Public progress updates. It also means having the hard conversations when someone falls short, *without delay*.

The biggest killer of team accountability? Inconsistency. Holding one person to the fire while letting another slide. Avoiding conversations because they're uncomfortable. That kind of leadership breeds resentment and confusion.

Accountability should feel like alignment, not fear. When people know where they stand, what's expected, and how to improve, they stop guessing. They start owning.

Coaching vs. Correcting vs. Cutting Loose

Not every performance issue means someone should be fired, but not every performance issue can be coached either. Leadership means knowing which tool to use, and when.

Coaching is for the people who are trying, but off track. They care. They want to grow. They're receptive to feedback, even if they're struggling to implement it. Coaching can also be about training, helping someone build the skills they don't yet have, not just correcting mistakes they've made. With coaching, you:

- Ask questions that invite reflection.

- Set small, clear next steps.

- Stay in dialogue, not monologue.

- Provide guidance, tools, and space to practice new skills.

Correcting is more direct. It's for moments when a boundary has been crossed or a behavior needs to change now. It sounds like:

- "This can't keep happening."

- "Here's the standard, and here's how you missed it."

- "This isn't about intent, it's about impact."

Correcting is still human, but it's firm. It sets consequences and expectations, and holds the line.

Cutting loose is the hardest, and often the most delayed. Sometimes however, someone is in the wrong seat. Maybe they're the right person for a different stage than the one you're in now, or they've simply shown, over time, that they can't or won't grow in the way the team needs.

Waiting too long to make that call is one of the biggest leadership mistakes. You don't just drain your own time. You lower the standard for everyone. Your team watches how you handle it. They know when someone isn't pulling their weight. If you let it drag, they learn that excellence is optional.

Letting someone go should be done with dignity and respect, but it should *be done.*

You can't build a strong team by holding on to the wrong players out of fear, guilt, or discomfort.

Coaching is generous. Correcting is necessary. Letting go, when needed, is leadership.

Reflection: What Kind of Team Are You Building?

- Who on your team lifts the culture, and who quietly drags it down?

- Where are you being too vague, or too passive, with expectations?

- What's one conversation you've been avoiding that could help someone improve?

- If you were being onboarded to your team today, what would confuse or frustrate you?

- What kind of leader would you want to be hired by, and are you being that person now?

Strong teams don't happen by accident. They're built, one clear hire, one honest conversation, and one strong standard at a time.

CHAPTER 21: THE DAILY PRACTICE OF NOT SUCKING

The best leaders aren't perfect. They're intentional, and consistent.

Let's get something clear right up front: this chapter isn't just for managers. It's for everyone: the CEO, customer service rep, new intern, tenured engineer, the front desk receptionist, even the remote freelancer. If you show up to work with other humans, this chapter is for you.

Because the truth is, you don't need a leadership title to act like a leader. You don't need a fancy org chart to develop the kind of daily habits that keep people from quietly avoiding you.

This is about *practice*. What you do consistently, not what you do when you're at your best. Not what you say in a team meeting, or what you post on LinkedIn. It's about what you repeat, especially when things get hard or messy and annoying.

You don't become a better teammate, a better communicator, or a better boss all at once. You become it in moments, in patterns, and in how you move through the day. Every day.

I want to give you tools, rituals, and reflection points that will help you *not suck* today, tomorrow, and the next day. Whether you're managing five people or managing just yourself, the principle is the same.

How you show up regularly becomes who you are.

The good news? You get to practice again every single day.

Leadership as a Daily Practice

Let's bust a myth right away: leadership is not some magical quality you either have or don't. It's not charisma. It's not confidence. It's consistency.

You become a better leader by practicing how you think, how you respond, how you speak, and how you recover, daily. This is the gym, and just like with fitness, missing one day doesn't kill you, but neglecting the reps over time absolutely will.

Again, this isn't just for people with a manager title. Even if you're not "in charge" of anyone, you're responsible for how you show up. You're still impacting the tone, trust, and clarity of every room you're in, even if that's virtually.

So what does a daily leadership practice actually look like?

- It looks like pausing before you fire off a snarky email.

- It looks like asking better questions instead of making assumptions.

- It looks like remembering that other people have a POV too (Chapter 3, anyone?).

- It looks like choosing to be calm, curious, and clear, on purpose.

It's not about being perfect. It's about building patterns. Patterns of behavior that make people want to work with you, not around you. Patterns that build trust, not tension.

When you make this a practice, when you decide to do the reps, everything starts to shift. You're not at the mercy of your moods. You're not spiraling every time something unexpected happens. You're becoming resilient, thoughtful, and intentional.

That kind of leadership? People feel it, and they remember it.

Emotional and Operational Hygiene

If leadership is a daily practice, then think of this as your daily hygiene routine. Just like brushing your teeth or taking a shower, this is how you stay clean, emotionally and operationally, so you don't start stinking up your team without realizing it.

Let's break this down further, because emotional hygiene is often confused with emotional intelligence.

Emotional intelligence (EQ) is your awareness and understanding of emotions, your own and others'. It's your ability to recognize emotional dynamics, empathize with people, manage your own reactions, and respond effectively. Think of EQ as the internal compass.

Emotional hygiene is what you *do* with that compass. It's the daily maintenance. The check-ins. Self-regulation. If EQ is your knowledge, emotional hygiene is your action. You can have high EQ and still show up messy if you're not practicing emotional hygiene.

Emotional hygiene means paying attention to how you feel and what you're carrying into the day. Are you tired? Resentful? Distracted? Triggered?

You don't have to be emotionless to be professional, but you do have to be self-aware. Emotional hygiene is about:

- Checking your mindset before walking into a meeting.

- Naming your feelings so they don't hijack your tone.

- Noticing when your ego is flaring up and taking a step back.

- Asking yourself, "Am I reacting to this person or something else entirely?"

If you've ever walked into a room and *felt* the tension before anyone spoke, that's poor emotional hygiene. One person walks in visibly agitated or off-kilter, and the entire team pays the price.

Operational hygiene is the clarity side of the equation. It's how you manage your commitments, your calendar, your clutter, so you're not showing up chaotic, scattered, or unprepared.

This includes:

- Reviewing your schedule and deliverables each morning.

- Clearing old to-dos and organizing what's next.

- Making sure your priorities actually match what's urgent and important.

- Saying "no" to the stuff that doesn't fit.

Great leaders don't run around pretending they're too busy to think. They know how to manage themselves, emotionally and operationally, so they can show up calm, grounded, and effective.

If emotional hygiene is about how you *feel*, operational hygiene is about how you *function*.

Clean both regularly, or things get gross.

The Daily and Weekly Reset

You're going to have off days. You're going to overreact. You're going to miss things. That's life, and that's work. What matters isn't perfection, it's the reset.

A solid daily and weekly reset isn't about adding more to your plate. It's about clearing it, so you can actually think straight, lead clearly, and avoid letting the emotional trash of today spill into tomorrow.

Daily Reset Prompts:

- **Morning:** "How do I want to show up today?"
  Before your first email, meeting, or coffee, check in. What kind of tone do you want to set? What does success *look* like today, not just in tasks, but in behavior?

- **Midday (or post-meeting):** "What did I bring into that room?"
  After high-stakes moments, reflect. Did you listen? Did your tone match your intent? Did you create clarity or chaos?

- **End of Day:** "What did I learn today?"
  Did you react in a way you regret? Did you step up in a way that surprised you? Did you avoid something important? That last five minutes of honesty helps you course-correct, and sleep better.

Weekly Reset Rituals:

- **Inventory your commitments.** Are you overbooked, undercommunicating, or spinning in circles? Time to recalibrate.

- **Check in with people.** Who haven't you talked to this week that you should've? Who needs feedback, praise, or clarification?

- **Reflect on alignment.** Are your actions and your role still aligned with your goals, your values, your energy?

This reset isn't about judgment. It's about ownership. If you're off track, reset. If you're on track, reinforce.

You don't build great leadership in a day. You build it in *the reset*.

Sometimes the hardest part of leadership, or just being a decent person at work, is remembering that you can't change what's already happened.

You can't undo a bad meeting. You can't take back a sharp comment or a dropped ball or a missed opportunity. You can't reverse a week (or month) where you totally lost the thread.

You *can* always reset.

That's the power of building a daily practice. Because no matter how off-course you were yesterday, you always have a new opportunity today. Emotional hygiene and operational clarity only work when we're future-focused. Not clinging to past mistakes or shame, but learning, adapting, and deciding to move forward with intention.

What's done is done. The question now is: what are you going to do next?

Reset. Re-engage. Repeat.

Self-Awareness Triggers and Patterns

If you've been paying attention throughout this book, one theme should be loud and clear by now: self-awareness is everything, and one of the most powerful ways to sharpen it is to learn your triggers.

Not just what *annoys* you, but what sends you into reaction mode. What makes you shut down, lash out, get passive-aggressive, or overfunction? What moments at work make you feel small, insecure, threatened, or overly responsible?

We all have these patterns. But most of us don't take the time to name them, and if you can't name them, you can't work with them.

Start by identifying the situations that regularly throw you off:

- When someone interrupts you in meetings.

- When you're left out of a decision.

- When your work goes unnoticed.

- When a deadline slips and no one seems to care.

Now ask: what do I *do* when that happens?

- Do I ruminate? Do I retreat? Do I blow up?

- Do I try to fix it all myself and spiral into martyrdom?

- Do I gossip? Do I vent to the wrong people?

Here's a personal example: One of my own triggers is the feeling that I've disappointed someone, especially a boss. If a manager says, "Can we talk?" without any context, my mind instantly goes to the worst-case scenario. I start assuming I did something wrong, even when I didn't. That's my perfectionism, mixed with my desire to keep everyone happy, rearing its head. Once I realized that pattern, I could name it. I could feel it coming, and I could start managing it.

That's what identifying triggers does. It helps you pause and think, "Wait. Is this situation actually dangerous, or am I reacting to an old narrative?"

Most of us think we're responding to the *moment.* Really, we're responding to a familiar *feeling* from some earlier experience that's being stirred up.

That's why this work matters. If you want to build daily habits that make you steady, thoughtful, and effective, you have to interrupt your own patterns.

Create systems that help:

- A post-meeting checklist: Did I show up the way I intended to?

- A colleague who can gently call you out when your pattern starts running the show.

- A moment of pause when you feel triggered: "Is this about now, or about something older?"

- Journaling brief notes when you feel off so you can look for repeated themes.

You don't have to fix everything overnight, but you do have to notice. Because what you don't notice, you will keep repeating.

Boundaries, Focus, and Saying No

We talked about boundaries in depth earlier in this book, and for good reason. If you want to be consistent, grounded, and effective over time, you have to be intentional about where your energy goes. This section isn't about introducing something new. It's a reminder: you cannot practice emotional or operational clarity without boundaries.

So, think of this as a quick audit:

- Are you still blocking time for focused work, or has your calendar drifted into chaos?

- Are you honoring your own limits, or saying yes out of guilt or fear?

- Are you modeling clarity with your time, or confusing responsiveness with availability?

Boundaries aren't about control. They're about sustainability. They allow you to stay present and useful *without* burning out. And they teach others how to engage with you, with respect, not assumption.

Leadership doesn't require martyrdom. It requires focus. The people who are best at what they do aren't the busiest. They're the ones who've learned how to say no with grace, so they can say yes to what really matters.

So take this moment to recalibrate. If you've let your boundaries slide, this is your reset.

Not because you're weak, but because you're wise.

Legacy Isn't Built on Big Speeches

We tend to think of leadership in highlight reels. The big speech. The bold move. The dramatic save. In reality, legacy, the impact you leave behind, is shaped by small, consistent moments.

It's built in how you handle yourself when no one's watching, how you respond when someone makes a mistake. It's built in the tone you set on a Tuesday morning when the pressure is high and the coffee's gone cold.

People don't remember everything you said, but they remember how they felt around you. Safe or scared. Heard or dismissed. Encouraged or overlooked.

Over time, those moments add up. A steady presence becomes a trusted voice. The person who stays calm when everything's on fire becomes the person others instinctively turn to. And eventually, you look up and realize, your legacy is already forming.

Want to know how to tell if you're on the right track? Ask yourself:

- Do people want to work with me again?

- When I leave a team, do they miss me, or breathe a sigh of relief?

- Do people I've led still reach out for advice, mentorship, or support?

I once spent a week in the hospital. Nothing dramatic, just one of those stretches where you have to hit pause whether you want to or not. When I came back to work, there was a giant card waiting for me, signed by over a hundred people. People I worked with across teams and across different levels. They were worried. They were happy I was back, and they wanted me to know.

That card cost nothing, but it meant everything. Legacy isn't about titles or achievements. It's about whether people care.

Every day, you build your legacy. With what you say, how you listen, how you recover from your worst moments, and show up better the next time.

The days you don't think about that? Those are the days your legacy starts to shrink.

So be thoughtful. Be steady. Be someone worth remembering.

Leadership isn't earned in the spotlight. It's built in the quiet, daily moments that no one applauds, but everyone feels.

Reflection: Practicing Not Sucking

- What's one small behavior I've repeated this week that I'm proud of?

- What's one reaction I'd like a do-over on, and what would I do differently?

- Where am I carrying emotional or operational clutter I need to clear?

- What system (daily or weekly) could help me reset and realign more consistently?

- Am I building a legacy I'd be proud of, one small moment at a time?

No one gets this perfect. That's not the goal. The goal is intention, repetition, and reflection. You don't have to master it all today, just commit to practicing.

Every day is another chance not to suck.

CHAPTER 22: DON'T JUST BE GOOD AT WORK. BE GOOD AT PEOPLE.

Business is human. Leadership is personal, and you are the culture you create.

Ok, let's land this plane.

You've made it through the hard truths, the uncomfortable reflections, and hopefully a few laughs along the way. If you've read this far, one thing is already clear: you care. You care about being better, and doing better. Not just surviving work, but actually making it better, for yourself and the people around you.

Here's a hard truth about the modern world: being good at *work* isn't going to be enough anymore.

Not when AI can write the emails, run the numbers, analyze the data, and maybe even do your job faster and cheaper than you can. Not when the next round of layoffs could come down to who makes the team stronger, safer, and more human. Not who gets the work done quickest.

You don't want to be just another box on a spreadsheet, because when it comes time to shrink the spreadsheet, those boxes disappear first.

The people who stick around? They're the ones who lead with empathy. The ones who make the team better. The ones who de-escalate drama, create clarity, build trust, and connect the dots between business and humanity.

In other words, the ones who are good at *people.*

This is the real work. The work that can't be automated. The work that defines how we feel about our jobs, our teams, and ourselves. The work that gets remembered when the dust settles.

We are not machines. We are not lines of code. We are people, complicated, emotional, ego-driven, fear-ridden, deeply flawed people. If we want to thrive in a world of increasing automation, then emotional intelligence, communication, collaboration, and courage aren't just "nice-to-haves." They're survival skills.

So don't just be good at what you do.

Be good at who you are.
Be good at how you show up.
Be good at people.

Because without that? None of the rest matters.

You've Made It This Far, Now What?

You've reflected on ego, fear, dysfunction, boundaries, burnout, feedback, and all the beautiful mess of working with other humans. You've examined your triggers, cleaned up your patterns, learned how to reset, and hopefully started to spot the behaviors that make a culture suck (or thrive).

You've done the work, and now you've got a choice: Let it sit on a shelf... or live it out loud.

Because once you've seen this stuff, you can't *unsee* it. You can't pretend dysfunction is normal. You can't go back to ignoring the things that drain your team or feed your resentment. You've named it. And now you're responsible for doing something with it.

The good news? You don't have to fix it all. You just have to take the first step.

The Work Isn't Finished, It Never Is

One of the biggest traps after a breakthrough is believing the work is done.

You read the book. You had the epiphany. You changed your behavior for a week. Then life happens. Pressure kicks in. Stress hits. You slide back into old habits, old tones, old reactions.

That doesn't mean you failed. That means you're human.

Growth isn't linear. Awareness doesn't make you immune. Self-development isn't about eliminating mistakes. It's about shortening the time between a misstep and a better response.

The real win? Catching yourself sooner. Recovering faster. Owning your impact before someone else has to call it out.

This work isn't about perfection. It's about *maintenance*.

Just like your body, your mindset, your communication, and your culture need daily care. When you stop tending to them, they decay.

This chapter isn't a wrap-up. It's a reset. A reminder that leadership is a practice, and the people who stay consistent, not flawless, are the ones who make the most impact over time.

So keep showing up. Keep checking your ego. Keep listening longer. Keep choosing clarity over control.

You don't need to be the finished product. You just need to keep becoming better.

The Most Important Job You Have: Modeling It

Here's the part that most people skip: all of this, the EQ, the communication, the boundaries, the resets, it doesn't matter if you're not modeling it.

People don't follow what you say. They follow what you *do.*

Want your team to take accountability? Model it. Want them to communicate directly and respectfully? Model it. Want them to own their growth and admit when they're off track? You guessed it, model it.

But it's not just about your work habits. Modeling leadership means modeling what it looks like to be a full, healthy human being. It means taking care of yourself in ways that aren't always obvious, but deeply important.

Want to lead better? Take care of your body. Take care of your mind. Stop drinking so much. Go to the gym. Take the damn walk at lunch. Actually use the mental health day. If you keep saying the work matters, then do *all* the work.

Leadership isn't just about what you accomplish. It's about what you normalize. If your team sees you burning out, chasing perfection, and skipping rest, they will do the same. If they see you move with clarity, own your mistakes, and take care of yourself, they'll start to believe they can too.

You're always modeling something. The question is: is it worth following?

Choose Your Impact (Whether You Mean To or Not)

Every day, you're shaping the environment around you, whether you mean to or not. Your tone, your decisions, your presence (or absence) is telling people something about what matters, what's acceptable, and what's expected.

You don't need to be in a leadership role to shape a culture. You do it just by showing up. Every meeting you join, every message you send, every moment you choose to speak up (or stay silent), it's all a signal.

You're either:

- Making things clearer or more confusing.

- Calming things down or ramping up the tension.

- Creating safety or creating fear.

That's not meant to pressure you, it's meant to *empower* you. Because no matter where you sit in the org chart, you have influence.

So take it seriously. Own your ripple effect. Ask yourself:

- How do people feel after interacting with me?

- What kind of energy do I bring into a room?

- What do I reinforce, even without saying a word?

Remember in the end, your legacy isn't built by the big moments. It's built in the hundreds of small choices you make when you think no one's watching.

But they are, and they're learning how to lead, or how to hide, based on what you do.

The Final Challenge: Be Someone Worth Following

So here's where we land: You don't need to be the smartest, most charismatic, or most senior person in the room. You just need to be someone who others *want* to follow.

Someone who:

- Listens more than they talk.

- Speaks clearly and directly.

- Owns their shit without turning it into a performance.

- Admits when they're wrong and gets back on track.

- Shows up with intention, not perfection.

You don't have to be a hero. But you do need to be honest, consistent, and real.

When it's hard, be steady. When it's tense, be clear. When others spiral, be grounded.

This is the work. This is the opportunity. This is what separates people who simply clock in and out from people who make a real impact.

It's not about being "liked." It's about being trusted. Respected. Remembered.

You won't always get applause. You won't always feel appreciated, but if you stay in it, if you keep practicing, the people who matter will see it.

They'll follow you. Not because they have to, but because they want to.

That's the kind of leader the world needs more of.

That's the kind of person worth becoming.

Reflection: Your Culture, Your Legacy

Take a breath. Look back, and ask yourself, what now?

Here's a simple daily habit that changed everything for me: Every day, instead of focusing on the 100 things on my plate, I just picked 3. Three things that mattered most. Three things I could actually get done. I let go of everything else, and just got focused.

You want to be successful? Start there. Every day, choose 3 things that move the needle, for your team, your mindset, or your legacy. Do them well. Then come back tomorrow and do it again.

Because you build who you are in the small, repeatable actions, not in the massive overhauls.

Ask yourself:

- What's the single biggest shift I've made (or want to make) after reading this?

- Where am I still playing small, safe, or reactive?

- What would it look like to model the kind of culture I wish existed, every day?

- Who do I need to apologize to, thank, or listen to more intentionally?

- If someone were learning how to lead by watching me, what would they learn?

This isn't just a leadership book. It's a mirror, and a challenge.

Be better, show up, and keep practicing.

Leadership isn't a title. It's the day-to-day choice to give a damn about how you impact the people around you. If you do that, really do that, you won't just be good at business.

You'll be unforgettable.

ABOUT THE AUTHOR

Ruben Buell

Business would be easy... if it wasn't for people.

That's the simple truth I've learned over 30+ years of leading companies, building technology, scaling teams, and yes, dealing with all the messy, frustrating, unpredictable humans along the way (including myself).

I'm Ruben Buell. I've been the CEO, the CTO, the startup founder, the corporate exec, the guy pulling all-nighters, and the one delivering bad news when things didn't go as planned. Through it all, I've seen firsthand that success in business (and in life) has less to do with being the smartest person in the room, and everything to do with how you lead, how you listen, and how you show up for others.

Why I Wrote Business Would Be Easy If It Wasn't for People

I wrote this book because I was tired of watching talented people crash and burn in leadership roles. I was tired of seeing companies with great products and smart strategies implode because no one knew how to manage the people side of the equation.

Most leadership books are too polished, too theoretical, or too full of corporate-speak. This one isn't. It's honest, practical, and built on real storie, my stories, and probably some of yours too.

What I Do Now

I live in Las Vegas with my family, my dog, two cats and a deep appreciation for good music, a day of golf, and people who don't suck.

I write, I lead, I consult, and I help people suck a little less at work and in life. Whether you're a first-time manager, a seasoned executive, or someone just trying to make it through Monday without losing your mind, this book is here to help.

www.ingramcontent.com/pod-product-compliance
Lightning Source LLC
Chambersburg PA
CBHW062057270326
41931CB00013B/3116